CUTOVER

IN SAP ACTIVATE®

Part 2 of the Guide: The Cutover
in SAP® projects

Waldemar Falinski

DGII WF

Copyright © 2024 Waldemar Faliński

All rights reserved

The characters and events portrayed in this book are fictitious. Any similarity to real persons, living or dead, is coincidental and not intended by the author.

No part of this book may be reproduced, or stored in a retrieval system, or transmitted in any form or by any means, electronic, mechanical, photocopying, recording, or otherwise, without express written permission of the publisher.

Cover Design and Figures in the Book by Waldemar Faliński
Library of Congress Control Number: 2018675309
Printed in the United States of America

CONTENTS

Title Page
Copyright
Disclaimer
Introduction to this Book — 1
1 Sources of information — 6
1.1 SAP Activate Roadmap Viewer — 7
1.2 SAP Community — 8
1.3 Web and AI Tools — 9
2 Terms and Artifacts — 10
2.1 SAP Projects, SAP Business Solutions — 12
2.2 SAP Activate — 13
2.3 The Cutover — 19
2.4 The Cutover Management — 24
2.6 Ramp-down and Ramp-up — 28
2.7 The Dress Rehearsal, Cutover Rehearsal, or Cutover Simulation — 30
2.8 The Cutover Dry Run, Walk-through — 32
2.9 The Blackout, Shutdown, and Downtime — 33
2.10 Freeze periods, Dual Maintenance — 34
2.11 The Mission Control Center (not War Room) — 35
2.12 The Definition of Go-Live — 36

2.13 (To-) Go-Live Weekend and Go-Live Day	38
2.14 Soft Go-Live	40
2.15 Golden Transactions, Smoke- and Penny-Tests	41
2.16 Business Continuity Plan	44
2.17 Emergency, Contingency, Rollback, and Fallback	46
2.18 Backup	48
2.19 The Point of No Return	50
2.20 The Hyper-Care	51
3 Roles and Teams	52
3.1 Project Manager and Cutover Manager	54
3.2 Stream Teams Engaged in the Cutover	56
3.3 Local Site Teams and Coordinators	59
3.4 Legacy System Persistence Team	60
3.5 External Teams Engaged in the Cutover	61
3.6 Sponsor, Senior Stakeholders	62
3.7 End Users	63
4 The SAP Activate Roadmap Journey	64
4.1 How to Use the SAP Activate Roadmap Viewer	66
4.2 The Process of Cutover Management in SAP Activate	68
4.3 About the Journey	70
4.4 Prepare	72
4.5 Explore	79
4.6 Realize – Start of preparation of the Cutover	83
4.7 Deploy – Cutover Preparation and Pre-Cutover	95
4.8 Deploy-Go/No-Go Decision and the Cutover	102
4.9 Deploy - Post-Cutover (Post-Go-Live)	112
4.10 Run	120
5 Quick Reference for Cutover Accelerators	121

5.1	How to use the Quick Reference?	122
5.2	General documents – blog posts by SAP Activate Team member	124
5.3	Cutover Accelerators	126
5.4	Other Accelerators that Touch the Cutover	131
5.5	Blog Posts for System Conversion and Optimizing the Downtime	135
5.6	Selective Data Transition and Landscape Transformation	137
6	Roadmaps and project plan templates	138
6.1	SAP Activate Methodology for Business Suite and On-Premise- Agile and Waterfall	139
6.2	SAP Activate Methodology for Transition to SAP S/4HANA	141
6.3	SAP Activate Methodology for the Intelligent Enterprise	143
6.4	SAP Activate Methodology for RISE with SAP S/4HANA Cloud Private Edition	145
6.5	SAP Activate for SAP S/4HANA Cloud Public Edition (3-system landscape)	146
6.6	Baseline Activation Service for SAP S/4HANA Cloud (3-system landscape)	147
6.7	SAP Activate for SAP S/4HANA Cloud Public Edition (2-system landscape)	148
6.8	Organizational Change Management	149
6.9	SAP Activate Methodology for New Cloud Implementations (Public Cloud-General)	150
6.11	SAP Activate Methodology for SAP S/4HANA Upgrades	152
7	Other useful links Within the SAP universe	153
	About The Author	155

DISCLAIMER

The information contained in this book is for informational purposes only. While every effort has been made to ensure the accuracy and completeness of the content provided, the author and publisher assume no responsibility for errors, omissions, or inaccuracies. The information presented is subject to change without notice and should not be construed as professional advice.

SAP Cutover processes and strategies can vary greatly depending on each organization's specific requirements, the complexity of the SAP system landscape, and the unique challenges encountered during implementation. The content in this book is based on the author's experiences and research and is intended to provide a general framework and best practices. However, it may not cover all scenarios or situations you may encounter.

Before applying any of the techniques or methodologies described in this book, readers are advised to seek professional advice and conduct thorough testing in a controlled environment. The author and publisher disclaim any liability or responsibility for any loss or damage that may arise directly or indirectly from the use of or reliance on the information contained in this book.

References to specific products, services, or companies are for illustrative purposes and do not constitute an endorsement or recommendation.

By reading this book, you agree that the author and publisher will not be held liable for any actions taken based on the information provided herein. Your use of any information or materials in this book is entirely at your own risk.
Please consult with qualified SAP professionals and consultants for detailed guidance and support tailored to your specific SAP implementation needs.

The trademarks and product names mentioned in this book are the property of their respective owners.
All the documents listed here should be accessible via the provided links even in anonymous mode (if not stated that the P-User or S-User is required). Efforts have been made to ensure their accessibility,

Please note that SAP Activate is an evolving framework, and the documents listed here may change, become unavailable, or be relocated over time.

The content in this book is based on the author's experiences and research. It is intended to describe SAP products and methods and provide links to documents published by SAP, which all remain the full property and copyright of SAP.

Note that even if these documents are declared public, they are still protected by the copyright of SAP.

This publication contains references to the products of SAP SE. SAP products and services mentioned herein as well as their respective logos are trademarks or registered trademarks of SAP SE in Germany and other countries.

SAP SE is neither the author nor the publisher of this publication and is not responsible for its content. SAP Group shall not be liable for errors or omissions with respect to the materials. The only warranties for SAP Group products and services are those that are set forth in the express warranty statements accompanying such products and services, if any. Nothing herein should be construed as constituting an additional warranty.

INTRODUCTION TO THIS BOOK

Welcome to **"Cutover in SAP Activate"**!

This is Part 2 of the series: **The Cutover in SAP® Projects – the Guide**

This book describes the Cutover Management process defined in SAP Activate, the official methodology for implementing SAP components like SAP S/4HANA, which creates Business Solutions.

I intentionally decided to limit my interpretations and possibly present this topic "as is." In the next book, I will extend it based on my best understanding and practice.

It includes a complimentary Quick Reference list of SAP Activate Accelerators and documents published by SAP to assist customers and partners with their SAP implementation projects, making this book a gate to a rich source of publicly available SAP Activate documentation.

This book is intentionally self-explanatory, but it may be helpful for you to read part 1, which examines the specific nature of the transition process called the Cutover. The links provided in this book give a fast path to studying all the related content of publicly available SAP Activate documentation.

Why Book about the Cutover in SAP Activate

This book explains the Cutover as defined and described

in SAP Activate, the project management methodology for implementing SAP component-based business solutions. The Cutover is the climax and most stressful part of every SAP implementation project. However, as explained in Part 1, this domain remains unsettled.

While the Cutover is mentioned in many components of SAP Activate, there is no consistent and structured description of it. The pieces are scattered across various workstreams, making it challenging to approach the Cutover consistently. This book aims to provide a structured description of the different variants, helping you manage and understand cutovers in your projects.

This book serves as an excellent starting point for those new to SAP projects while offering fresh insights and navigation tools for experienced professionals.

SAP Activate is the benchmark for Every SAP Implementation Method

Today, many SAP projects utilize proprietary implementation methods, but SAP Activate remains the benchmark and reference for all these methods. This makes the book relevant not only for SAP projects but also for non-SAP ERP projects.

It's important to note that all SAP Activate content is publicly available, making this book a key to accessing this rich vault of knowledge and artifacts.

SAP Activate is the official methodology for implementing SAP S/4HANA business solutions. It's called a framework because the methodology is just one of its three pillars.

Although it may not be as popular as ASAP was in the past, SAP Activate is still invaluable for SAP and other ERP implementations, setting the standard for all SAP business solutions deployments. SAP Activate components—such as the Accelerators listed in this Quick Reference—can easily integrate into any proprietary corporate methodology used in SAP S/4HANA projects.

One significant advantage of SAP Activate is its publicly available content. The Roadmap Viewer is the primary tool for accessing this content, which contains hundreds or thousands of resources.

Why the Quick Reference List here

The main challenge with using SAP Activate is that it is designed for various types of SAP deployments and is continually updated and expanded. As a result, many "roadmaps"—essentially specific methodologies—create a hierarchical and multi-level structure.

While this diversity is beneficial, it can also be complex and challenging. Moreover, documents are sometimes not assigned optimally. For instance, the roadmap for Organizational Change Management might lack assigned accelerators, while many relevant accelerators are found in other roadmaps.

While helpful, the Roadmap Viewer's search tool is not perfect. It finds objects containing the given text but may miss specific items, such as "`PP_010`" (a project plan in a zipped file).

Given these challenges, navigating and finding all the relevant documents can be difficult. This was my experience, and that's why I believe this Quick Reference will be helpful to you. It made me a more efficient navigator in my SAP Activate journey, and I'm confident it will do the same for you.

Who is this Book for?

In discussions with my colleagues, I've noticed that many people are unaware that SAP Activate is publicly accessible and contains a wealth of valuable content.

This book offers an opportunity to learn and explore the

practical aspects of the Cutover in SAP business solutions implementation projects as described in SAP Activate. It can be helpful for anyone who is a stakeholder or potential stakeholder in an SAP project, regardless of the project's scope or environment.

Because the SAP Business Solution implementation is a sound case of what we call "Digital Transformation," this book may be beneficial for anyone interested in or influenced by Digital Transformation.

This introduction and Quick Reference List are precious for:

- SAP Project Managers
- Cutover Managers or Leads
- Members of SAP (or widely ERP) project teams
- All leads and managers of teams within any SAP projects
- Business managers in all project areas of SAP projects
- SAP project stakeholders
- IT teams
- Business students

All documents are declared public but hold SAP's copyright, which means your relationship with SAP matters.

Please also refer to the disclaimer in this book.

Prerequisites for reading this Book

While this book is part of a series, you do not need to read the other parts to understand. It is designed to be independent of the topic, providing the necessary introductions.

However, familiarity with the earlier part may provide additional context about the nature of the Cutover and give the overview of the entire series creating The Guide. The following parts extend the topic of this book.

You may want to learn more about SAP Activate, but the publicly available content in the SAP Roadmap Viewer can be a valuable resource for self-study. This book provides an explanation of how to use it.

Disclaimer

All the documents listed here should be accessible via the provided links even in anonymous mode (if not stated that the P-User or S-User is required). Efforts have been made to ensure their accessibility,

Please note that SAP Activate is an evolving framework, and the documents listed here may change, become unavailable, or be relocated over time.

The content in this book is based on the author's experiences and research. It is intended to describe SAP products and methods and provide links to documents published by SAP, which all remain the full property and copyright of SAP.

Note that even if these documents are declared public, they are still protected by the copyright of SAP.

This publication contains references to the products of SAP SE. SAP products and services mentioned herein as well as their respective logos are trademarks or registered trademarks of SAP SE in Germany and other countries.

SAP SE is neither the author nor the publisher of this publication and is not responsible for its content. SAP Group shall not be liable for errors or omissions with respect to the materials. The only warranties for SAP Group products and services are those that are set forth in the express warranty statements accompanying such products and services, if any. Nothing herein should be construed as constituting an additional warranty.

1 SOURCES OF INFORMATION

SAP Training and Books

I have worked as a project manager and cutover manager on SAP projects for decades, so I ground the content presented here in practical experience.

I am well-versed in the available SAP training and literature, and I have utilized these resources while writing this book.

This is particularly true for the ACT100 training, which is the core training for the SAP Activate Methodology. ACT100 provides comprehensive information about SAP Activate, including its elements, workstreams, and foundational scenarios. This training serves as a rich resource for understanding SAP Activate. As a trainer for this course, I conduct sessions at the SAP Training Center in Warsaw.

However, I have chosen to primarily rely on publicly available resources for this book, specifically the SAP Roadmap Viewer, the roadmaps published there, and the SAP Activate Accelerators that complement these roadmaps. This approach ensures you have full and immediate access to all content and references in this book.

1.1 SAP ACTIVATE ROADMAP VIEWER

As said, the wealthiest and most up-to-date sources of SAP Activate knowledge are:

- The publicly available portal SAP Roadmap Viewer
- The roadmaps published on this portal
- The SAP Activate Accelerators, which complement and are attached to these roadmaps

Here is a guide on how to use the SAP Activate Roadmap Viewer: https://roadmapviewer-supportportal.dispatcher.hana.ondemand.com/#/getStarted

The Roadmap Viewer includes a search function that allows you to search for text within the hierarchy and navigate through the hierarchical structure. However, this way, you cannot find documents by name.

To access the accelerator, if you know the name of the file (exact with extension), you can add it to the end of the path:

https://support.sap.com/content/dam/SAAP/SAP_Activate/

like for FP_44.xls: https://support.sap.com/content/dam/SAAP/SAP_Activate/FP_44.xls

This way, however, does not work for all accelerators as some are located in other spaces.

1.2 SAP COMMUNITY

SAP also declares that the SAP Community (an ancestor of the previously available SAP Jam) is an official SAP Activate specification and knowledge source.

Here is the link to "SAP Activate" space:

https://community.sap.com/topics/activate

There are blog posts from SAP Activate team members that can be helpful and reliable sources.

Some of these blog posts are linked within SAP Activate as Accelerators. I will include some references to some most interesting for the cutover here.

1.3 WEB AND AI TOOLS

To validate my concepts, I have browsed the Web and consulted my statements with the following AI tools:

- PMI Infinity 1.0
- ChatGPT
- Gemini

Occasionally, I also used to cross-check:

- Perplexity
- COPILOT
- Claude

I used all of these tools in their free versions.

I also utilized the premium version of Grammarly to ensure that the text was clear and readable in English, which is not my native language.

2 TERMS AND ARTIFACTS

This section focuses on the Cutover in any SAP project that implements components forming the SAP Business Solution.

To help with understanding, I've employed metaphors throughout the guide. In Part 1, I introduced two key metaphors:

- heart transplant surgery: the cutover starts with the first incision and takes till the new heart starts beating.
- space missions: the cutover begins with the launch and takes till a safe landing.

Both metaphors highlight critical aspects:

- **Time pressure and teamwork:** Many people are involved in real-time, under tight time constraints, making communication essential.
- **Cutover's criticality:** It's difficult to pause or reverse the process once started.
- **Disruption to IT and business:** The cutover is a disruptive process for the technology solutions and thus may be disruptive for business operations

Cutover – Like a Space Mission to the Moon

An SAP project is like a space mission to the Moon: after lengthy preparation, the cutover is akin to launching the spacecraft. In this metaphor, the Go-Live is comparable to landing on the Moon's surface. While reaching the target is important, the highest priority is the crew's safety. Similarly, business safety is paramount in an SAP cutover, and this must be considered carefully when making the "To-Go" decision.

The SAP Business Solution Involves Multiple Components...

... Returning to the space mission metaphor, the cutover might involve simultaneously launching multiple "space shuttles" (i.e., SAP components). Some may launch together, while others launch sequentially. This complexity introduces numerous challenges that will be explored later in this book.

For simplicity's sake, we'll focus on one cutover scenario here.

Given the large number of people involved and the importance of clear communication, this chapter's merit lies in defining key terms related to the cutover.

2.1 SAP PROJECTS, SAP BUSINESS SOLUTIONS

SAP Business Solutions combines SAP components, third-party components, and integrations with external business partners, customers, vendors, and other service providers. This may include outsourced aspects of the business, such as sub-manufacturers or external storage providers.

SAP S/4HANA is typically the most complex and central component of these solutions, serving as the backbone around which other components are built. While S/4HANA may be implemented on-premise, many additional SAP components are often available only in the cloud and sometimes exclusively in the public cloud model. In on-premise implementations, the focus is primarily on the central ERP component, alongside possibly a few other SAP or third-party components.

SAP projects refer to any implementation based on SAP technology (usually S/4HANA) that aims to build a particular SAP Business Solution. Depending on the scope, components, and business requirements, these projects may vary in complexity.

2.2 SAP ACTIVATE

The story that led to SAP Activate has been described in Book No. 1 of this Guide; here are just some characteristics necessary to understand the methodological context of the Cutover.

SAP Activate is named the framework as the methodology is one of three elements, also called pillars. The remaining two are Tools and Predefined Content.

This book will mainly discuss predefined content (such as Accelerators) and the methodology that prescribes what to do, when, and by whom.

2.2.1 Phases

Time-wise, SAP Activate is structured into project phases with 6 phases, but only 4 out of 6 are project phases. Briefly:

1. "Discover phase": This phase is about discovering the value of the new SAP Business Solution, possibly along with elaboration of the Business Case document, which forms the foundation of the decision to start the SAP implementation project.

2. "Prepare phase": This phase formally starts the project. Organizationally, it begins for all stakeholders with the Kick-Off meeting, which launches the plan and all the project work.

3. "Explore phase": The main activity here is the validation of the prototype setup based on best practices or a model company. Depending on the roadmap, a Fit/Gap or Fit-to-Standard approach is applied for any new implementation. This phase ends with the defined solution to be realized. In the case

of a system conversion, the existing custom code needs to be analyzed in terms of SAP S/4HANA readiness.

4. "Realize phase": This phase involves realizing the solution with a suite of functional tests.

5. "Deploy phase": This phase involves preparing to go live, the cutover to production, and post-cutover activities. It marks the end of the project.

6. "Run phase": This phase is about business as usual of the newly implemented SAP Business Solution along with stabilization and optimization of the implemented solution.

Please review the drawing, noting that I have adjusted the phase durations to match what is commonly presented in SAP Activate documentation. As shown, the Execute and Realize phases are more than twice as long as the Prepare and Deploy phases, which aligns with what I've observed in practice. This highlights the compressed timeline for Cutover and Cutover Management.

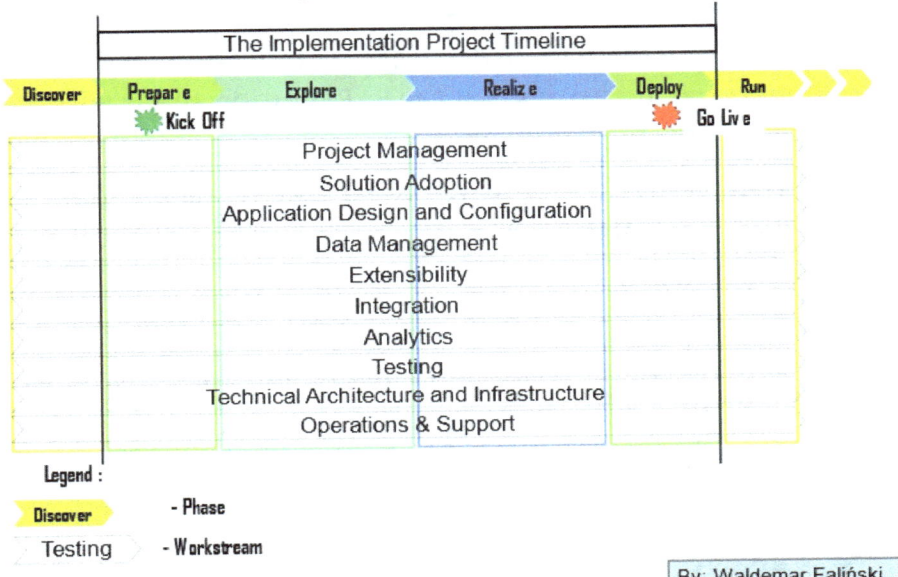

Figure 2.1: Diagram showing the fundamental structure of SAP Activate

2.2.2 Workstreams

Another dimension of the methodology is workstreams. Workstreams group the activities, deliverables, and artifacts. Here's a brief overview of the key workstreams:

- **Project Management:** This workstream covers project preparation, planning, and execution. It often follows a "two in the box" approach, meaning there are two project managers: one representing the vendor and one the customer.

- **Solution Adoption:** This workstream is focused on organizational change management (OCM). It includes enabling and training the project team and developing strategies and learning paths to prepare end users to use the SAP business solution effectively.

- **Application Design and Configuration:** This workstream involves identifying and designing functional changes using a Fit/Gap or Fit-to-Standard approach. It ensures that the SAP solution aligns with functional requirements.

- **Data Management:** This workstream manages many of the cutover activities and is responsible for migrating or converting business data.

- **Extensibility:** Focused on creating or converting custom extensions and ensuring that customizations are compatible with the SAP solution.

- **Integration:** This workstream ensures integration within the SAP solution and external systems.

- **Analytics:** This workstream addresses the analytics requirements for the project, ensuring necessary insights are available.

- **Testing:** Covers the planning and execution of various tests, including integration, regression, and user acceptance testing.

- **Technical Architecture and Infrastructure:** This Workstream focuses on planning and setting up the SAP solution's hardware, infrastructure, and technical elements.

- **Operations & Support:** Prepares for the ongoing maintenance and support of the live SAP business solution.

Currently, there are 10 primary Workstreams, potentially 11, as Enablement is sometimes presented separately from Solution Adoption.

2.2.3 Quality Gates

The important component of the methodology is Quality Management, which is implemented through Quality Gates. The minimal set includes five gates, four of which occur at the end of each project phase, and one extra gate before the Cutover begins.

In essence, Quality Gates functions similarly to PMI's Tollgate Methodology, ensuring a structured, phased approach to project management with a strong focus on quality, stakeholder involvement, and continuous improvement.

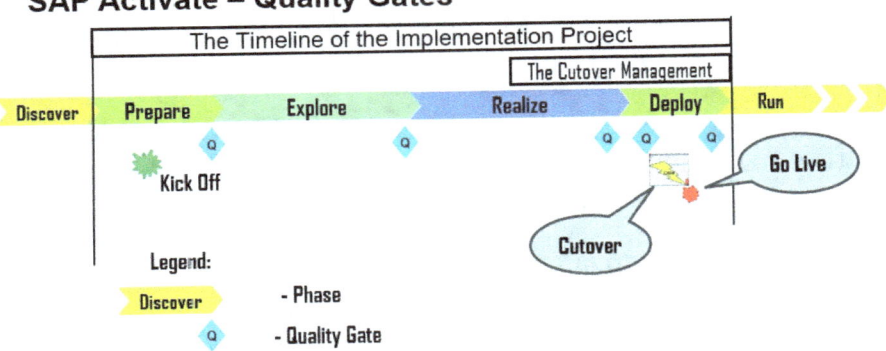

Figure 2.2: Diagram showing the Quality Gates in SAP Activate

Quality Gates are meetings of the Steering Committee where the project manager and other managers present the project's current state. They must orally defend the progress made to date.

The Accelerator `PM_210.pptx` further explains the concept of Quality Gates. Two accelerators featuring questionnaires (the older `PM_210` and the newer `S4H_0271`) must be prepared for these meetings. All points must be addressed before proceeding to the next phase.

SAP Activate assumes a 'happy flow"

Projects would achieve perfect cutovers and go-lives if all quality criteria were fulfilled.

However, this is seldom the practice case when it comes to the Cutover, which must be carefully prepared to mitigate risks caused by unmet quality criteria. The next book will cover case studies, while future books on Emergency and Continuity will provide further insights into these aspects.

2.2.4 Conclusion

This structure forms the foundation of the roadmap, but there are various roadmaps in SAP Activate.

In the previous methodology, ASAP (Accelerated SAP), there was only one roadmap. SAP Activate offers multiple roadmaps tailored to different project scenarios.

There are currently 28 roadmaps, but this number is continuously evolving. For this book, I've selected the most representative roadmaps.

While each roadmap is named after a specific scenario or group of scenarios, it is recommended to explore multiple roadmaps. Every project is unique and may involve elements from various roadmaps, and this approach is reflected throughout this book.

If this brief description of SAP Activate isn't enough, refer to the detailed explanation of all phases and components in the SAP Activate Roadmap Viewer (link available in the Quick Reference section).

2.3 THE CUTOVER

When discussing the cutover, it's often assumed to include the entire Cutover Management process, with the cutover itself being the culmination point. In this section, we will focus on the cutover process, while the following subchapter will cover Cutover Management in more detail.

The cutover refers to the transition of business operations from a legacy IT system to the new SAP S/4HANA solution. It has clearly defined start and end points.

Using a metaphor of a space mission, after long preparation, the decision to launch is made, followed by the final countdown and the actual launch. This marks the beginning of the cutover process.

Here's a definition of cutover based on SAP Activate documentation:

> **The cutover is the process ...**
>
> **... of switching a company's business operations from one system to another.** It involves both technical and business aspects. This marks when the old system is shut down and before the new system becomes operational. The transition period, where no IT system supports business operations, creates time pressure, distinguishing the cutover from any other typical transition.

In SAP Activate, a Quality Gate is tied to this decision (e.g., Accelerator **S4H_0271**), and once initiated, the cutover usually cannot be reversed unless significant issues arise. Sometimes, the cutover begins with the first significant activity targeting the production system, such as moving configurations of new business units into the new system.

Nevertheless, the cutover officially starts at a predefined and communicated point, making it a crucial milestone on the path to the new business solution.

Cutover as a Heart Transplant Metaphor

The cutover process can be compared to heart transplant surgery. It begins with the first incision (the "Go" decision), following thorough patient preparation. Similarly, the organization is prepared, and the system's state is stable enough to begin the transition. These preceding activities are the planning and pre-cutover steps.

The cutover continues until the new heart (the new system) starts beating, representing the Go-Live. Afterward, the focus shifts to stabilizing the system (post-cutover), just as a patient would go through rehabilitation. Cutover Management encompasses everything from preparation to stabilization, leading to the Go-Live and handing over to normal business operations.

Although this sounds straightforward, the cutover is a highly specific and complex transition. The reasons for using this type of transition in SAP projects and the unique characteristics of the cutover are explored in detail in Part 1 of this guide. Below is a simplified diagram of the cutover process:

2.3 THE CUTOVER

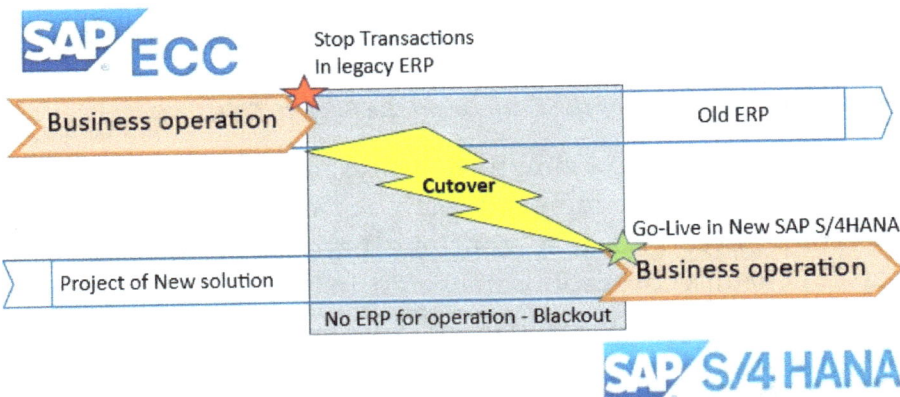

Figure 2.3: Simplified diagram showing the SAP Cutover

This diagram provides a basic overview of the cutover. It works for many scenarios but may not be accurate for all. The cutover typically leads through a blackout period, during which business operations are paused, but the timing may vary. In some conversion scenarios, there is only one system environment instead of two, which can shift the timing.

This scenario illustrates a New Implementation. End-user access ends at the "Stop Transaction in legacy ERP" point, after which the old ERP system is no longer used.

For conversion projects, the old and new systems are technically the same.

During the cutover (often called the "Cutover Weekend"), no ERP system is available, leading to downtime.

This period includes data migration, switching productive integration flows, and granting access to the new system. Typically, there are many more activities during this phase.

The cutover concludes with a successful Go-Live. At this point, the new SAP S/4HANA system will become operational.

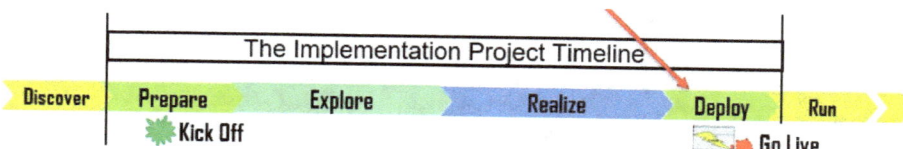

Figure 2.4: Placement of the Cutover on the Project Timeline

This diagram shows a simplified representation of the cutover. In practice, it is far more complex. For example, some legacy system transactions may continue beyond the Go-Live, and certain business operations may start in the new system before the cutover is fully completed.

Expanded Definition of the SAP Cutover

The SAP Cutover is the climax of the implementation project, occurring near its end. It represents the transition of business operations from an old IT system to a new SAP ERP-based solution. This process involves complexity and requires the business to be accountable for the outcome. The transition must be fast while also ensuring business continuity and safety.

Though the cutover seems like a simple transition, the challenge lies in its complexity, which varies depending on the project.

Key Characteristics of the Cutover

- The cutover introduces significant changes, bringing a new IT system into live operation and leading to adjustments in business processes.

- The cutover must be completed swiftly to minimize downtime without compromising safety.

- Numerous interdependent activities from various project streams must be executed within a limited timeframe to avoid operational disruptions.

- The cutover requires the involvement of many people, including occasional stakeholders.

- It leads to and concludes with a successful Go-Live.

- Careful planning, thorough testing, and close collaboration between IT and business teams are essential for a smooth cutover.

It's important to note that one key prerequisite for cutover, as checked at the Quality Gate (**S4H_0271**), is ensuring that all preceding activities have been completed and that all expected deliverables meet quality standards

2.4 THE CUTOVER MANAGEMENT

Now, we have arrived at the broader process of Cutover Management.

An older Quality Gate Checklist Accelerator document, **PM_211.xlsx**, provides the following definition of Cutover Management:

"Covers planning and execution of activities to cutover the system into production including the hyper-care support period shortly after cutover"

We can outline the following stages of Cutover Management, which may align with project phases:

1. **Preparation and Pre-Cutover**
2. **Cutover until Successful Go-Live**
3. **Post-Cutover, leading to the Handover of the New System to Operations**

Below is an illustration showing an example of the cutover in the context of the Cutover Management process:

2.4 THE CUTOVER MANAGEMENT

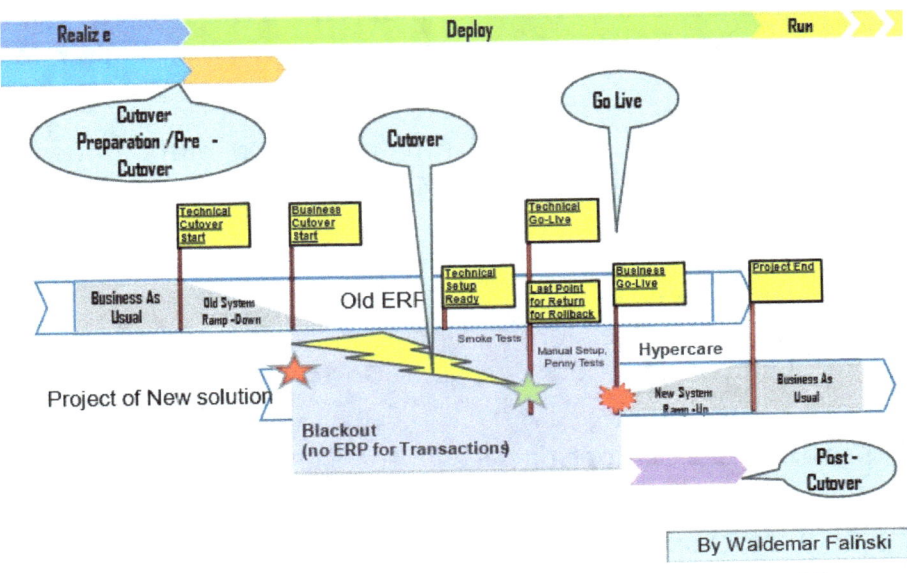

Figure 2.5: The Example of SAP Cutover in the broader context of Cutover Management

Subsequent parts of this book will cover the details of these steps, including the event that marks the beginning of the Cutover. Here is a picture showing the entire Cutover Management as defined in SAP Activate in the context of the entire project cycle.

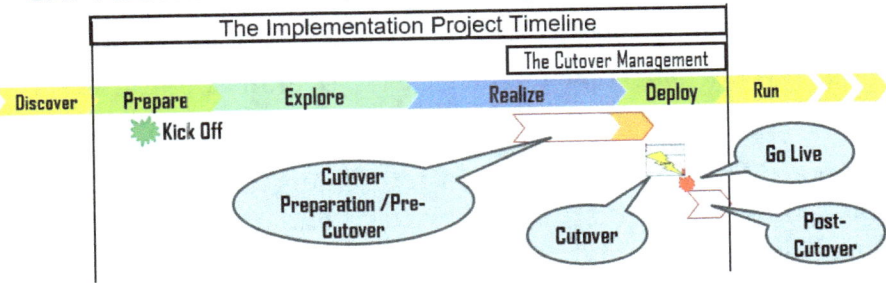

Figure 2.6: Steps of the Cutover Management in SAP Activate

This picture presents the main concept of Cutover Management, which is also found in many other places of the SAP Activate content: that Cutover Management commences in mid- or end-of-the Realize phase and lasts until the end of the project. Please see the initial section of the "Roadmaps journey" chapter for more.

In the Accelerator "**S4H_747**" we can see a more in-depth breakdown that the Cutover Management consists of the following 5 steps:

- Cutover Planning
- Dress Rehearsal
- Go/No-go Decision
- Final (Production) Cutover & Go-Live
- Post-Cutover Activities

Note that in the case of this Accelerator, the above bears the label "remote" because it adds some typical remote context. However, today, all the cutovers are at least partly remote, so it does mark the Cutover Management in SAP Activate.

2.5 *The Cutover Plan, Schedule, Runbook, etc.*

Several plan templates are available, which we will review further in this booklet.

The **Cutover Plan** is typically a subset of the broader Project Plan, and the Cutover Manager oversees its execution.

In SAP Activate, as noted in the Accelerator "**S4H_747**," it is advised that the Cutover Plan can be distributed to local teams for large, multi-site, or multi-country projects. However, a master Cutover Plan ensures that overall integration and alignment remain intact.

Cutover Schedule is often used interchangeably with **Cutover Plan**, but subtle distinctions exist. The **Cutover Schedule** generally refers to highly detailed intervals within the Cutover process, typically broken down into hours or even minutes, especially where tightly coordinated activities must occur concurrently under time pressure.

While the **Cutover Plan** is often structured in days, the **Cutover Schedule** is time-sensitive and may focus on minute-by-minute execution during critical phases.

Other terms synonymous with Cutover Schedule include:

- Cutover Runbook
- Cutover Playbook
- Cutover Workbook
- Cutover Cookbook

The cutover plan does not need to detail the level captured in the Schedule; if necessary, it can keep some major activities, but in general, the Schedule will take control of execution for the time being.

2.6　RAMP-DOWN AND RAMP-UP

As part of the cutover preparation, the business must ramp down its operations, which can be considered part of pre-cutover activities or even as part of the cutover itself if the technical cutover has already begun.

One critical aspect of this preparation is **ramping down operations** and closing as many activities as possible in the legacy system before leaving that environment. This process is similar to typical end-of-month or end-of-year closings, but **Ramp-Down** must be broader and more thorough before the transition. Typical Ramp-Down activities include:

- **Cleansing and removing obsolete data** to minimize the data migration volume.

- **Closing open orders**, as in some cases, it may be preferable to reopen them after the transition rather than relying on data migration.

In the next book, we will discuss the golden rules of cutover. One rule is to minimize business transaction volume during the cutover. This requires proactive communication with business partners to ensure they are aware of potential disruptions.

Sometimes, bypassing certain internal processes during the blackout period may be necessary to continue business operations. For example, temporary external storage may be used to ensure uninterrupted customer service.

Ramp-up is the opposite process that occurs after going live. The business must cautiously increase its operations to avoid compounding issues or creating more significant problems due to incorrect data.

Issues are often expected immediately after going live. We will address this topic in detail in the book about Business Emergency. For now, it is sufficient to note that the business should resume operations cautiously, and total operational capacity may take some time to achieve. This process is referred to as **Ramp-Up**.

This is also illustrated in **Figure 2.3**.

2.7 THE DRESS REHEARSAL, CUTOVER REHEARSAL, OR CUTOVER SIMULATION

In SAP Activate, the terms Dress Rehearsal, Cutover Rehearsal, and Cutover Simulation are used interchangeably to describe the full practical test of the cutover process.

According to Accelerator **BB_158**, **Cutover Test** is defined as:

"The Cutover test phase will verify all go-live processes including the technical and functional system deployment, business verifications and processes such as reconciliation, data conversions or migrations with production volumes and production data and finally confirm installation/cut over time window"

The SAP Activate methodology suggests that the **Dress Rehearsal** be performed during the **Deploy** phase, shortly before the Go/No-Go decision and the actual cutover.

Dress Rehearsal in the Deploy phase is a challenge...

However, due to time constraints, conducting this full-scale test at such a late stage may be challenging. There are several reasons why this can be difficult to achieve in practice. Given the scope and complexity of modern SAP S/4HANA projects, which often involve multiple components, executing a full-scale Dress Rehearsal is time-consuming and resource-intensive. All activities should be carried out efficiently, following established project management principles.

As a result, some projects skip the full-scale dress rehearsal or perform it only partially.

2.8 THE CUTOVER DRY RUN, WALK-THROUGH

In SAP Activate, an exercise helps prepare for the Dress Rehearsal and, consequently, the Cutover. For example, the advice on performing the Dry Run can be found in the Accelerator "**S4H_747.**"

The Dry Run is an oral walkthrough of the plan. All teams should participate, and the assigned person should read aloud and make comments on the activities. This is a relatively inexpensive but very effective exercise

2.9 THE BLACKOUT, SHUTDOWN, AND DOWNTIME

As previously mentioned, the Cutover process is often accompanied by a Blackout period when the ERP system is unavailable for business.

This period is sometimes called Shutdown or Downtime, but these terms may carry different technical connotations. For example, a Blackout might begin on a Friday afternoon, but the legacy system could still be operational while the technical team works on preparations. At some point, the legacy system may be shut down for specific reasons. However, this is not the same as the Blackout itself. In fact, the legacy system could remain operational throughout, with write access restricted, making it available for reference purposes only.

During this time, the old system is blocked for users, and the new system remains locked until it's fully enabled. Weekends or holidays are usually preferred for this transition, as they coincide with periods of lower business activity. However, in some cases, the Blackout may extend beyond a weekend, lasting a week or even longer. If the business cannot afford to remain idle during this time (as it would during holidays), a Business Continuity Plan must be developed to ensure continued operations.

2.10 FREEZE PERIODS, DUAL MAINTENANCE

In addition to a complete blackout, certain activities may experience periods of partial lockdown, such as when data in the old system must remain unchanged after extraction.

Dual Maintenance can be used during the freeze period to allow continued operations. For instance, if data has already been extracted from the source system and migrated to the new system, but the source system remains operational for a time. This situation typically occurs in Pre-Cutover or Cutover scenarios, where the data volume requires loading well before the actual transition.

One example of Dual Maintenance (here considering configuration but similarly may be data), called also the Retrofit, is a passage in the Accelerator **Transition_to_SAP_S4HANA - 24Q1_Final**:

"Please note: In case of a system conversion, the old DEV system will stay for production support of PRD if PRD is not converted. Take care to properly retrofit changes performed in the production support landscape to the new DEV system to ensure the latest business requirements are accounted for within the project landscape."

2.11 THE MISSION CONTROL CENTER (NOT WAR ROOM)

SAP Activate introduces an interesting concept called the "Cutover Mission Control Center." This concept is primarily related to SAP's implementation assistance services and should ideally be applied during the cutover phase of complex projects.

In some documents, this is referred to as a "war room" or "crisis room"—a naming convention that is quite popular in project management. However, as I prefer a more positive naming approach, I will use the term "Cutover Mission Control Center."

This describes a coordinated way of working during cutover periods that require synchronization and control. If conducted on-site, key individuals may gather in the same room, similar to NASA's Mission Control Center setup during a space launch. This is especially relevant for cutover events where the schedule is tight, and many activities must be executed concurrently quickly.

> **I am against terms like "The War Room" ...**
>
> ...because, during the Cutover, we are not engaging in a war.
>
> Likewise, calling it a "Crisis Room" is inappropriate, as we are not managing a crisis. Such names can create the wrong perception and foster a negative attitude. Instead, I advocate for the more positive and constructive term "Mission Control Center," inspired by space missions.

2.12 THE DEFINITION OF GO-LIVE

Defining Go-Live may seem straightforward. In earlier SAP implementation methodologies, it was simply a moment when the new system went live.

However, in practice, it is more complex today. Go-Live is usually seen as a designated point in time to communicate the start of operations in the new solution to all stakeholders. This is often referred to as the Go-Live point.

> **The Go-Live (point) ...**
>
> ... is used to inform stakeholders, but in practice, it represents a broader process that begins before this point, often called the Go-Live Window or Go-Live Weekend, and includes a ramp-up phase afterward—usually the first day, known as Go-Live Day. The conclusion of the cutover generally marks the success of the Go-Live process.

Typically, the Go-Live point is set at the beginning of the first working day following the Go-Live Weekend and is communicated to stakeholders, often accompanied by a formal kick-off event.

In some cases, a technical Go-Live is distinguished from the full Go-Live. In this stage, the business solution may be operational (verified through smoke tests), but additional activities are still needed to ensure the solution is fully business-ready. This may involve manual setup of the Business Solution (like opening periods, etc.) but also so-called penny tests, where select real-time processes with actual data are executed in a controlled environment.

From this point, a sequence of technical and business activities must be performed to ensure that the expected scope of processes is running smoothly. The solution's functionality is confirmed by executing a set of real end-to-end processes (penny tests). Often, at the end of the first day (Go-Live Day), the authority overseeing the project, typically the Steering Committee, acknowledges that the Go-Live has been successful.

Since the Go-Live marks the start of operations, and the activities after it continues prior efforts (such as penny tests and business setup), it is logical to include the Go-Live within the scope of the Cutover.

2.13 (TO-) GO-LIVE WEEKEND AND GO-LIVE DAY

The last days of the cutover phase, just before the Go-Live, are often called the Go-Live Window or Go-Live Weekend, as this typically happens over a weekend. More accurately, this period could be called the "To-Go-Live Window" or "To-Go-Live Weekend" since it leads to the actual Go-Live.

Here is an example of a typical Go-Live sequence, often encountered in cutovers:

Cutover Step	Activities
End of Friday before Go-Live Weekend	Decision to proceed (Go / No-Go) for the Go-Live
Go-Live Weekend (starts after Go decision)	The old system is blocked for users (Blackout), final setups and data migrations occur; smoke tests (technical validation) and penny tests (business validation) are performed; decision to proceed with Go-Live
Go-Live (Monday at 7 am)	Kick-off event confirming the Go-Live sequence
Go-Live Day (Monday)	Performing the sequence of activities to ramp up the business operation in the New

	Business Solution
End of Go-Live Day (Monday)	Decision on whether the Go-Live is successful; conclusion of Cutover and transition to Hypercare (Post-Cutover)

Table 2.1: Example of model SAP Go-Live sequence

> **Note: We will only cover the "happy flow" here**
> We will only cover the "happy flow" scenario here, and contingency plans will be discussed in another book in this series.

During this period, a blackout typically occurs, during which the old system is blocked for users but before the new system is fully enabled. Weekends or holidays are preferred for this transition, as they often align with periods of low business activity.

While limiting the blackout to a weekend is ideal, it is crucial to schedule this transition in a way that minimizes disruption to business operations.

Throughout the Go-Live weekend, various cutover activities are performed, including transporting customizations, final data migrations, and integrating all necessary components for the Go-Live. These activities culminate in smoke tests (technical checks) and penny tests (selected business transactions). On Monday morning, the Go-Live is officially declared, allowing at least the first wave of users access to the new system.

However, even after the Go-Live is declared, much must be done. An apt analogy is a factory where machines need time to warm up. In this sense, the Go-Live process continues throughout the first full day.

2.14 SOFT GO-LIVE

The term "Soft Go-Live" in SAP Activate (as seen in the Accelerator "**S4H-747**") has three meanings:

- Parallel run of old and new business solutions for a certain period.

- Performing transactions without committing the changes to the system's data state.

- Releasing the new business solution to some users to check the quality in a controlled environment.

The first approach is now considered obsolete and rarely feasible. Due to tight system integration and data requirements, maintaining two systems in parallel is impractical. This is why Cutover is necessary today, involving a transition period with a gap (referred to as the Blackout) between shutting down the old system and starting the new one.

The second option has limited value because it doesn't allow us to fully evaluate the transaction logic without committing changes. This method only provides a superficial sense that the system is functioning correctly. We refer to this type of activity as a "Smoke Test."

The third option involves performing end-to-end testing in a controlled environment. This means releasing the newly implemented system to a small group of users who, under supervision, carry out real business transactions using real business data. We refer to this kind of test as a "Penny Test."

I keep an eye on the last two options as practicable today.

2.15 GOLDEN TRANSACTIONS, SMOKE- AND PENNY-TESTS

Continuing on the concept of the "Soft Go-Live," the second and third options lead to two stages of testing after the Go-Live.

It is important to remember that these tests are conducted in the business solution's production environment (PRD).

All actions in the PRD have lasting consequences

Important: All actions performed in the PRD environment have lasting consequences. The production system is a live business operation environment designed for reliability, where all changes are permanent and auditable. Even though the term "test" is used, any data modified in PRD cannot be undone, so extra care must be taken.

These two stages of testing are to be carried out by business users authorized to work in the live environment:

- **Smoke Test:** This involves performing operations that do not alter the system's transactional data state to verify that the system appears to be functioning as expected.
- **Penny Test:** This involves executing complete end-to-end transactions, including committing transactional data changes, but in a controlled and low-risk manner.

While the Smoke Test can be done quickly, in about 30 minutes, the Penny Test should be performed cautiously and sequentially to minimize the risk of any damage.

> **The term "Smoke Test" originates from the hardware industry**
> ... It refers to powering up a newly assembled device during its final assembly phase to check for any malfunction, such as smoke indicating a severe issue.

In software, the term has been adapted with a similar idea—to bring the system up and quickly check for potential problems, though not actual smoke.

In the software context, the Smoke Test does not alter any data in the PRD. A typical example is when the Cutover Manager instructs all users participating in the test to log in and view the screens they will use in their daily work. They may change master data but not any transactional data.

The Smoke Test is intended to provide a quick system check, often in a short window like 30 minutes, as outlined in the Cutover Schedule. All users report their findings, allowing the Cutover Manager to assess the system's state before proceeding to the next activity.

Once the Smoke Test is complete with a positive result, the next stage begins: the Penny Test is conducted.

> **The term "Penny Test" comes from the banking industry**
> ... It involves transferring minimal money—a "penny"—to verify a bank account connection.

The concept remains the same in ERP software testing, but it focuses on executing full business processes. One penny will make a difference in the balance; thus, a real business transaction with minimal associated risk is recommended for SAP Business Solutions Cutovers.

It has been adopted in the software industry with a slightly different meaning. It is still about end-to-end business processes, but it does not necessarily matter about the minimal amount. It shall be a real business operation, but it will not matter much if that fails. That has to be decided in the context of the business. For example, selecting operations that can wait for the fix without considerable pressure for their completion.

> **What's worse than wrongly migrated data?**
>
> The results of transactions performed on that incorrect data. If you've heard of systems that, even months after Go-Live, still require corrections for errors, it's likely due to issues compounded by transactions executed on incorrectly migrated data. This is why Penny Tests are so important.

These tests are often about the scope of so-called **Golden Transactions**, a set of critical transactions or functions that must be verified first to ensure the system is correctly configured.

2.16 BUSINESS CONTINUITY PLAN

A Business Continuity Plan (BCP) is a document for any organization that outlines strategies to address potential situations that may disrupt operations. These situations can range from natural disasters to technical failures like power outages to expected and planned changes.

A BCP is also important in the context of an ERP cutover due to the cutover process's inherently disruptive nature and associated risks.

By definition, the cutover process leads to discontinuity and disruptions in ERP services, potentially impacting business continuity. These disruptions may involve downtime, data migration challenges, or user access limitations, which can affect the business's normal operations.

Provided the organization already has BCP, it may also be extended to the event to cover the Cutover challenges.

As said, Business Continuity Plans typically encompass two key layers in the context of the Cutover:

- **Emergency Planning:** This layer focuses on immediate actions to respond to any problem during the Cutover. IT may be extended to the Post-Cutover as the Hyper Care is logical continuation of the special care put during the Go-Live.

- **Business Continuity for the Time of the Cutover:** This

layer outlines strategies to maintain critical business functions and minimize disruptions when ERP access is limited or unavailable.

These aspects will be described in the books in this Gude series, whereas the book about business continuity will focus on the second aspect. It may be that the setup is fortunate, and the entire Cutover fits into the Cutover Weekend window, which means no business activity is supposed to happen now. If it is not so, and for the time of Ramp-Up, then complete Blackout (no ERP support at all) and then Ramp-down there is a wish to safeguard the business operation, the Business Continuity Plan is needed providing the means and interim processes, as shown in the picture:

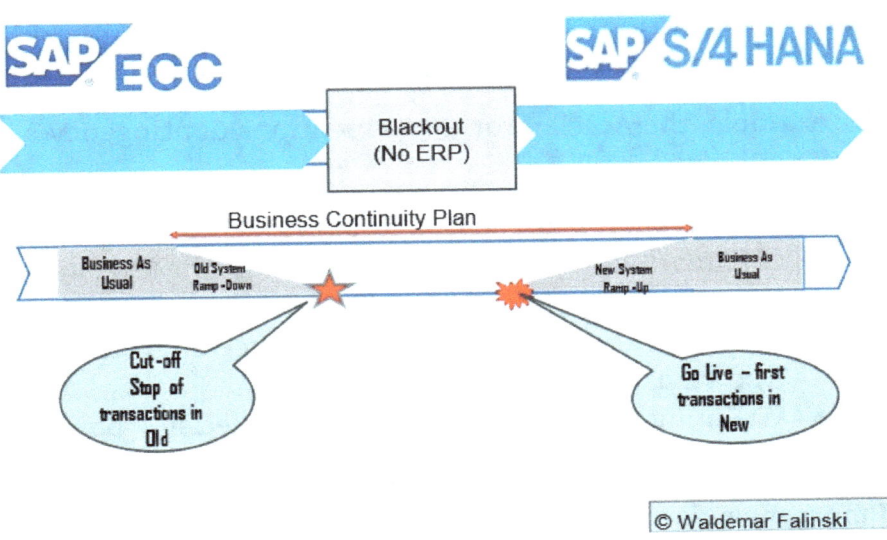

Figure 2.7: Diagram illustrating the challenge to keep the business ongoing in time of restricted and no access to ERP

Below are just some keywords related to BCP.

2.17 EMERGENCY, CONTINGENCY, ROLLBACK, AND FALLBACK

These terms appear in SAP Activate documents as measures to mitigate risks when something goes wrong. Additionally, other related terms may also be used, such as:

- Restoration of the Legacy
- Failover (which is a kind of automated Fallback)

For example, the Accelerator R-169 mentions Contingency as a set of activities:

- Identifying risks and mitigations for cutover
- Estimating the time required to restore the legacy system
- Determining decision points for proceeding with the next steps
- Defining acceptance criteria for each decision point

I will use this standard definition to explain all aspects of **Emergency Planning** in the next book of this series:

- **Contingency**: An overarching plan that includes actions to continue operations in case of issues. It may involve temporary workarounds and specific steps if continuation is impossible and an emergency exit (recovery) is required.

- **Fallback**: A temporary recovery action to switch to an alternative system or process. It generally involves discontinuing the current action with the option to resume after the necessary time for fixes has passed.

- **Rollback**: A discontinuation and escape action to revert to a previous, stable state of the system or environment, usually involving the complete abandonment of the cutover attempt.

- **Workarounds**: Temporary solutions that allow operations to continue until a permanent fix is implemented.

2.18 BACKUP

In SAP Activate documentation, the term "backup" frequently appears in two distinct contexts:

- ◆ As the common method for ensuring the continuous operation and recovery of the ERP system.
- ◆ As a safeguard specifically for the Cutover process.

This Guide focuses on the second context, which has particular considerations that differ from the typical data security and recovery scenarios.

It's important to note that a backup alone is not a complete recovery solution; it serves as one component of a broader emergency plan. An SAP Business Solution typically consists of numerous interconnected elements (collectively forming the SAP Standard Environment), and recovery from an ERP backup must account for all these components to ensure full system functionality.

> **Example: Middleware Upgrades**
> Certain technical components, such as interfacing middleware, may need to be upgraded during the cutover. If a backup is restored, any changes introduced during the upgrade—such as middleware updates—must be reversed to return the system to its previous state. This requirement should be explicitly included in the Emergency Plan.

As a best practice, which will be discussed further in the next book, it is advisable not to bundle too many changes with the SAP Cutover, as doing so can introduce additional risks and complicate emergency planning. This is why bundling the SAP Cutover with any technical Release is not recommended.

It is worth mentioning that relying solely on a backup as an emergency plan is often an illusion. A comprehensive S/4HANA-based solution is far too complex to revert simply by restoring a backup. Additional activities are usually required, and the backup recovery process can fail, especially if it has not been thoroughly tested.

> **A poorly planned emergency response can be worse...**
>
> ... A poorly planned or outdated emergency response can be worse than no plan. Consider the Chernobyl catastrophe a sobering example: the goal was merely to test something in production. However, when the test went wrong, they relied on an outdated rollback plan that had not been updated in years. This decision contributed to turning a manageable problem into a major disaster.
>
> The same principle applies to SAP projects. Some believe that having a system backup is sufficient. While this may have worked in simpler systems of the past, today's environments are much more complex. Restoring a backup for just one component in an interconnected environment may not be enough to restore full functionality.

Fortunately, in my experience, a complete rollback has never been necessary. Despite significant challenges, contingency options and workarounds have enabled us to continue moving forward.

2.19 THE POINT OF NO RETURN

A key aspect of Emergency Planning is establishing decision criteria and specific points at which critical decisions must be made. One such milestone in the Cutover plan is the Point of No Return, which marks the last point where recovery or rollback to the old system is possible. Typically, this is based on economic considerations regarding the effort and cost required to revert to the previous state.

A contingency plan should always be in place for emergencies. The Point of No Return is the designated moment after which, should the situation deteriorate significantly, any attempt to retreat to the old system fully must be carefully controlled.

It's essential to understand that the cutover process progresses until this point, which can also be seen as the point of a successful Go-Live. At this critical juncture, the team must make a final, controlled decision: either proceed with the cutover and transition to the hyper-care phase (post-cutover) or, if necessary, revert to the old system.

Typically, this decision is based on business and technical evaluations of the effort required to roll back. The Steering Committee or a designated decision-making body assesses the situation at this point, usually during the middle or end of the Go-Live day.

The details of Emergency Planning will be discussed further in a future volume of this guide.

2.20 THE HYPER-CARE

After the successful conclusion of Go-Live, the project continued, though it shifted its focus to actual business operations in the New Business Solution. This period is often referred to as **Hyper-Care.**

Usually, this is along with the Ramp-Up, where the intensity of operations is below full scale but gradually increases to normal levels.

During this phase, the project team typically provides special, fast-tracked support to the business as it adjusts to the new system. However, this additional support may vary depending on the project's requirements.

The main criterion for concluding the project and transitioning to regular maintenance is the system's stability, often measured by resolving incidents that arise during this final project stage.

3 ROLES AND TEAMS

Many documents of SAP Activate, such as Accelerators R_169 and FP_45, name or describe the roles and teams involved. Here, I compile based on many documents the teams and roles relevant to the Cutover Management process.

"Two in the Box" Concept

In SAP projects, the "Two in the Box" concept refers to the idea that certain management or leadership roles may be filled by two individuals—one from the vendor's side and one from the customer's side.

This dual-role setup results from the close collaboration between the vendor's consulting team and the customer's business team. It acknowledges the need for consultants to often remain isolated from real business data while ensuring that key customer users are deeply involved in preparing the new business solution.

This concept was introduced in the first book of this guide and is briefly mentioned here to explain why certain roles may be "duplicated." This duplication reflects the different functions and focuses of a project's customer and vendor representatives.

Project Manager is the role that almost every project undergoes this concept. Typically, the two individuals filling this role have distinct focuses or responsibilities:

- The person from the vendor side usually manages the

technical or consulting aspects of the project.

- The person from the customer side focuses on the business needs, ensuring that internal processes and key users are aligned with the project goals.

The leading project manager is usually from the vendor's side, focusing on delivering the solution, while the customer's representative may focus on organizational change management (OCM), ensuring that the business adapts to the new solution effectively.

This concept can be applied to other managerial roles in SAP projects. For instance, two Cutover Managers may collaborate and report together:

- One Cutover Manager from the system integrator's side, coordinating consultants.

- One Cutover Manager from the customer's side, coordinating key users and local Cutover Coordinators at subsidiary locations

3.1 PROJECT MANAGER AND CUTOVER MANAGER

The Cutover Manager role, sometimes called the Cutover Lead, is the most important part of this book's discipline. It has been extensively covered in Part 1 of this guide, and here, we expand on it further.

Cutover Management is a subdomain of project management, and in smaller projects, the Project Manager may also take on this role. However, following best practices, it is recommended that these roles be distinguished.

Cutover Management involves complex, cross-stream activities and coordination, similar to project management. Unfortunately, Cutover Management is not recognized as a distinct domain in SAP Activate, and related artifacts are scattered across various streams.

A clear and still-relevant definition of the Cutover Manager's role can be found in the one-pager from the previous methodology, ASAP (Accelerated SAP), dated January 9, 2010. I cite it here in full:

"*Description*

The cutover Manager is the key person in planning all aspects of the cutover and providing support to project manager and integration managed during the cutover. The person playing this role must pay attention to every detail of the cutover, he/she needs to be very experienced in planning large projects with large number of moving parts. It is also important for this person to be detail oriented, good communicator and experienced in managing medium to large teams.

Key Tasks

- *Provide guidelines and support for cutover planning and organization*
  - *for business topics*
  - *for technical topics*
- *Provide template for detailed cutover plan*
- *Knowledge transfer about all transition tasks (content, dependencies, timing)-> enable local cutover managers to plan and prepare their go-lives*
- *Follow up execution of go-live preparation activities in local organizations*
- *General support for local cutover managers"*

From this, we can identify key characteristics of the Cutover Manager role:

1. The Cutover Manager must possess strong soft skills, including communication, organization, mentoring, and team-building to create dynamic teams.

2. Since cutovers may occur across multiple locations or units simultaneously, local cutover leads and a central Cutover Manager must coordinate the entire process.

3. The cutover process has two layers—technical and business. This aligns with the "Two in the Box" concept, where one Cutover Manager handles the business side, and the other (typically from the vendor) manages the technical side. Close collaboration between both is critical for success.

3.2 STREAM TEAMS ENGAGED IN THE CUTOVER

Almost all workstreams, as defined in SAP Activate, are involved in the cutover process, with some having a stronger focus and impact than others. The key streams typically involved in the cutover include:

- **Solution Adoption Stream** (commonly referred to as the Organizational Change Management (OCM) team)
- **Application Design and Configuration**
- **Integration**
- **Extensibility**
- **Data Management**
- **Technical Architecture & Infrastructure**
- **Operations and Support**
- **Testing**

These teams are organized in workstreams. Their leads often reflect the "Two in the Box" concept, where representatives from both the vendor (consultants) and the customer Subject Matter Experts (SMEs) collaborate. In addition, third-party representatives may be involved, particularly for integrating third-party components.

3.2.1 Stream Leads

As said Stream Leads can follow the "Two in the Box" model, especially in case of complex streams like Data, and in complex projects. Taking Data stream, they play a critical role in cutover activities, with one of the most challenging tasks being final data migration, including delta loads and configuration transfers to the production (PRD) instance.

However, other stream leads also have a stake in the cutover process, managing their respective areas to ensure a smooth transition.

3.2.2 SAP Consultants

SAP Consultants provide expert advice and experience, particularly in projects like the transition from SAP ECC to SAP S/4HANA. While 20 years ago, the vendor typically unified and provided the consultant group, today, it often includes a mix of external and internal consultants.

In companies that have long used SAP ECC, internal consultants often form a **Competence Center**, which SAP Activate refers to as the **Center of Excellence (CoE)**.

Internal consultants may also play dual roles, acting as consultants, Subject Matter Experts, and/or Process Owners.

3.2.3 Key Users, Subject Matter Experts, etc.

Business specialists are delegated from the business side to take responsibility for the SAP deployment within their respective units and execute project tasks. Their roles may include:

- **Key User**
- **Power User**
- **Subject Matter Expert (SME)**
- **Process Owner**

◆ **Product Owner**

These individuals are key players in the cutover, working closely with end-users to ensure successful execution.

3.3 LOCAL SITE TEAMS AND COORDINATORS

The cutover process ultimately takes place within individual business units, meaning that it must be executed at each site in large, multi-site projects. This means that besides the business representatives working in "central" streams, business specialists are needed for local implementation in every site.

While efforts are typically made to standardize the entire solution, project, and cutover process across all locations (in line with overall project standardization), some sites may require a tailored approach due to their specific needs. Therefore, local coordination is essential.

This need for local coordination is reflected in various parts of the SAP Activate methodology, such as in the Accelerator **R_169**.

In some cases, the Site Coordinator for the cutover may be the local project lead. However, in more complex locations, hiring or appointing a Local Cutover Manager or Lead may be beneficial. Their responsibilities might include:

- Managing site readiness
- Managing the local cutover plan and schedules
- Managing site-specific issues and overseeing their resolution

3.4 LEGACY SYSTEM PERSISTENCE TEAM

This team is referenced, for example, in the Accelerator **FP_45**. Typically, the Legacy System Persistence Team is part of the technical workstream; however, in some cases, they may operate independently from the main project structure, coordinated only through a service agreement.

It is essential to highlight this team here because they play a significant role in the technical aspects of the cutover. They are sometimes involved in business-related tasks, such as data extraction and cleansing.

3.5 EXTERNAL TEAMS ENGAGED IN THE CUTOVER

In many projects, SAP components are integrated with non-SAP systems. Representatives from the vendors of these systems are crucial for the success of the cutover, especially when interface or integration issues need to be resolved.

External teams involved in the cutover may include:

- Service providers for non-SAP integration middleware
- Specific cloud service providers
- Outsourced providers of certain business processes
- External storage, transportation, sub-production partners, etc.

The Cutover Manager is responsible for coordinating with these external teams' leads, aligning on the activities to be completed, and addressing any time-critical integration dependencies.

3.6 SPONSOR, SENIOR STAKEHOLDERS

The project sponsor and key business decision-makers are crucial in the cutover preparation and execution. These senior stakeholders significantly influence the process, as they are often responsible for making critical decisions, including the final go/no-go decision for the go-live.

Their involvement may include:

- Monitoring the progress of the cutover to ensure alignment with business goals.
- Providing strategic guidance and support when needed.
- Serving as the escalation point for quickly resolving issues that cannot be addressed within the project's standard structure.

The sponsor, in particular, acts as the primary escalation body, ensuring that any high-priority concerns are addressed swiftly. Thus, it facilitates smooth cutover execution and minimizes disruptions.

3.7   END USERS

End Users, a specific group of SAP users, typically become involved later in the project. Their primary engagement usually begins during the **End-User Training** phase and continues post-go-live when they use the system in their day-to-day activities.

While most of their involvement is after going live, there may be cases where certain individuals from this group participate in specific cutover activities. This can include tasks such as:

- Providing feedback during user acceptance testing (UAT).
- Assisting with system validation during the cutover process.
- Participating in limited data verification or system checks to ensure readiness.

Their participation is crucial for ensuring a smooth transition, as they will be the system's primary users once it is live.

4 THE SAP ACTIVATE ROADMAP JOURNEY

The SAP Activate Roadmap Viewer is the official tool for accessing the knowledge and content of SAP Activate. You can find the SAP Activate Roadmap Viewer at the following link:

https://roadmapviewer-supportportal.dispatcher.hana.ondemand.com/#

This comprehensive, hyperlinked portal contains a wealth of content, primarily organized into roadmaps. These roadmaps are variants of SAP Activate tailored for specific implementation scenarios.

These roadmaps are publicly accessible, allowing users to explore the many predefined roadmaps available. Additionally, the viewer includes links to blog posts by members of the SAP Activate team, which are considered official knowledge sources. Various templates, documents, and guides, known as "Accelerators," are also accessible.

In general, SAP explains the content of this tool in its "Terms of Use" (https://support.sap.com/en/terms-of-use.html), I cite:

"...articles, information, data, code, text, SAP software or related documentation, documentation and product specification, application program interface specifications, concepts, designs, programming techniques and programming concepts, flow charts,

graphics, images, training and other services as well as marketing material around SAPs products and services"

I will guide you through the Cutover journey using the various roadmaps in this chapter. My primary reason for doing so is that the Cutover content is spread across different streams, artifacts, documents, portals, etc., and my guidance will make it easier for you to navigate.

First, we need to introduce the Roadmap Viewer itself.

4.1 HOW TO USE THE SAP ACTIVATE ROADMAP VIEWER

There are three levels of access to the content of the SAP Activate Roadmap Viewer:

- ◆ Anonymous – with very wide access, I would say it gives access to 80%, maybe even 90%, of the content.

- ◆ Personal User (P-User)— This access may be available to anyone interested in SAP Activate. It provides access to project plan templates, usually in ZIP files.

- ◆ SAP User (S-User): This is intended for customers and partners. Objects with access only for this group are marked yellow in this book.

For more detailed guidance on how to use the Roadmap Viewer, refer to the following link: https://roadmapviewer-supportportal.dispatcher.hana.ondemand.com/#/getStarted

The Roadmap Viewer also includes a search function, which allows you to search within the hierarchy in addition to navigating through the structured roadmap. You can access the search tool here: https://roadmapviewer-supportportal.dispatcher.hana.ondemand.com/#/searchResult/Cutover/roadmapGuids//types

However, learning how to use this tool effectively may take some time. For example, you cannot search for documents by their names, which requires some practice in navigating the platform.

This is why I've created this Quick Reference: to gather all the links directly leading to Cutover-related accelerators. It has been helpful in my work, and I believe it will also be useful to many of you.

4.2 THE PROCESS OF CUTOVER MANAGEMENT IN SAP ACTIVATE

The concept of Cutover Management is extensively described in various SAP Activate documents. It was also introduced earlier in this book in the section on terminology. Now, we will explore how it is structured as a process.

Cutover Management activities "officially" begin midway through the Realize phase and extend beyond Go-Live, continuing until the end of the project, which corresponds to the conclusion of the Deploy phase.

This is explicitly outlined, e.g., in the "**SAP Activate Quality Gate Concept (Public)**" Accelerator **PM_210.pptx**, valid for all roadmaps.

The diagram presents a simplified Cutover Management process consisting of three key steps:

- **Cutover Preparation** may include some early cutover activities known as **Pre-Cutover**.
- **Cutover**, including the **Go-Live** event.
- **Post-Cutover**.

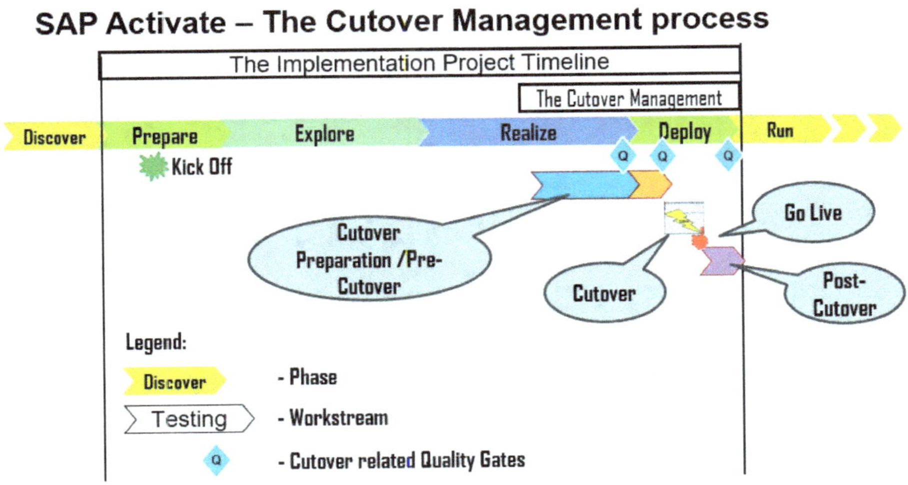

4.2 THE PROCESS OF CUTOVER MANAGEMENT IN SA... 69

SAP Activate – The Cutover Management process

Figure 4.1: Diagram illustrating the SAP Activate Cutover Management concept

The cutover management process originated during the early days of SAP R/3 and the earlier ASAP methodology. It was thoroughly explained in Part 1 of this guide and in the earlier section on cutover and Cutover Management definitions.

The description above outlines the main concept of Cutover Management in SAP Activate, but you will see that it also happens a lot before the official start of mid-Realize. Activities related to Cutover Management are also located in earlier phases and, in some cases, extend beyond the end of the project.

As an example of this kind of deviation, I will name it the Accelerator **S4H_747 How to Approach Remote Cutover.pptx**. This document, also called "Playbook for Remote Cutover" in some places, comes with some cutover activities that enter the Run phase.

4.3 ABOUT THE JOURNEY

SAP Activate Roadmaps are one of the richest sources of information about Cutover in SAP projects. However, as mentioned earlier, this content is scattered across various streams and documents, making implementing a consistent Cutover Management process somewhat challenging.

While some documents, such as the Quality Gate Checklist mentioned above, are consistent across all roadmaps, the presentation of Cutover activities can vary depending on the roadmap. There are also some notable exceptions to the general Cutover concept.

For this reason, I will walk you through the phases by presenting the concept as it appears in several representative roadmaps I've selected.

> **Tip: SAP recommends exploring multiple roadmaps...**
>
> ...even if some roadmaps seem to be designed for different scenarios, they may contain useful information. For example, a roadmap labeled "Cloud" may still offer valuable insights for an "On-Premise" application, and the "Upgrade" roadmap may be beneficial for conversion scenarios.

In many instances, SAP encourages users to browse various roadmaps and assemble content that best suits their needs. This book mirrored this approach, where I combine content from multiple roadmaps.

The roadmaps I am referring to include:

- SAP Activate Methodology for Business Suite and On-Premise (Agile and Waterfall)
- SAP Activate Methodology for Transition to SAP S/4HANA (focused on On-Premise)
- SAP Activate Methodology for RISE with SAP S/4HANA Cloud, Private Edition
- SAP Activate Methodology for New Cloud Implementations (Public Cloud - General)

By progressing from the oldest and most general roadmaps to more specific ones, I can present the most comprehensive path for managing Cutover activities. Links to these roadmaps are in the Quick Reference section of this book.

You can find more about the roadmaps itself in the chapter, which presents roadmaps and project plan templates attached to these roadmaps.

Cutover is a cross-stream process involving all stakeholders, including those responsible for business, data, and system readiness. The activities presented below are assigned to various workstreams. Since this book's view is cutover-centric, I will not show this assignment to make the picture simple and clear. You can trace it yourself using the links given.

We begin this journey with the **Prepare** phase, as I haven't found any cutover-related content in Discover, which is the phase preceding the start of the project.

4.4 PREPARE

Prepare is the first project phase in SAP Activate. I have selected activities from two Roadmaps to present here.

All these tasks described below have plenty of sub-tasks, and their localization in the project timeline is similar to the last figure (4.2).

4.4.1 SAP Activate Methodology for Transition to SAP S/4HANA

In this Roadmap, even if "officially" the Cutover Management starts at the end of Realize, there is a Cutover task located in Prepare: **Define Cutover Approach**

> For the Roadmap: *SAP Activate Methodology for Transition to SAP S/4HANA*
>
> Task: **Define Cutover Approach (High Level)**
>
> https://go.support.sap.com/roadmapviewer/#/group//roadmap/S4HANATRANSONPRE/node/001999B7BD851ED68D81408968ACC2CE:
>
> The description of this task is below.
>
> The following Accelerator with some interesting mentions about the Cutover is attached to this task (please find in the Quick Reference section – this is the lessons-learned document:
>
> **SAP S/4HANA Conversion in Finance**

4.4 PREPARE

This task is part of the node "Transition planning"

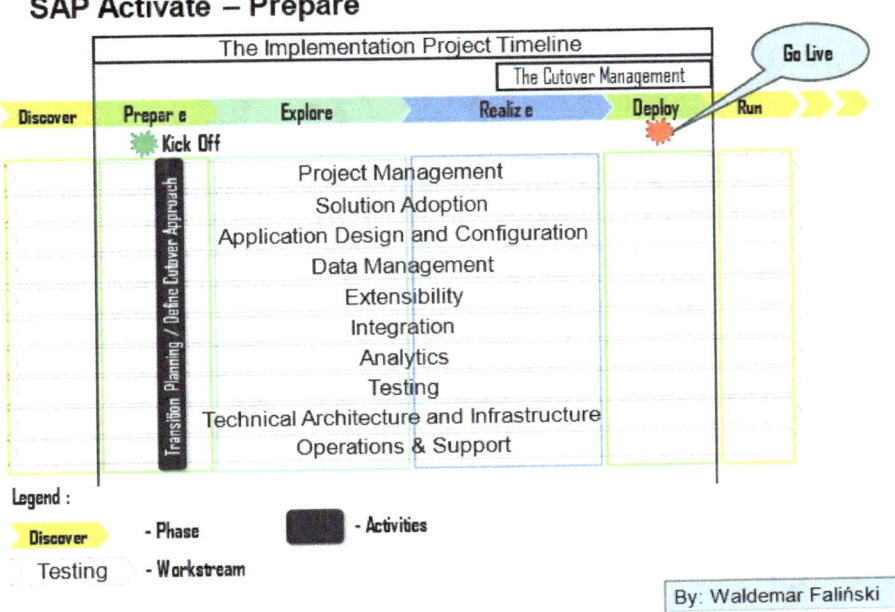

Figure 4.2: The task Define Cutover Approach (High Level)

This task comes with comprehensive specifications here in the Roadmap. The description of this task commences with the statement:

'The cutover approach for system conversion and new implementation differs.'

This is important and obvious, but this Roadmap is generally unified for all three transition paths.

This task comes with comprehensive specifications and diagrams for both the named paths.

Just a note that it mentions that the Cutover often happens on weekends, thus introducing the term 'Cutover Weekend.':

"Cutover" is the process of bringing the SAP S/4HANA system

into a productive state. This is often done on weekends ("Cutover weekend", Go-Live") at Go-Live. However the activities may start weeks before"

4.4.2 SAP Activate Methodology for RISE with SAP S/4HANA Cloud Private Edition

In this Roadmap, the Cutover starts very early and is very intensive. Prepare includes multiple activities that may be classified as Cutover Preparation, even to the level of some testing and proofs of concepts.

That is why we need to focus only on the most apparent cutover-related activities.

There is a node called **Transition Planning** with multiple Cutover related activities:

For the Roadmap: *SAP Activate Methodology for RISE with SAP S/4HANA Cloud Private Edition*

Activities Node: **Transition Planning**

There are at least two activities that are Cutover related:

- ◆ Define Cutover Strategy
- ◆ Perform Data Volume Planning

Activity: **Define Cutover Strategy**

https://go.support.sap.com/roadmapviewer/#/group//roadmap/a11ec6d657054bf9:FA163EAF25B21EEB8FC47DE9E72888DB/node/FA163EAF25B21EDB95A017E5BB467DBE/FA163EAF25B21EDB959FFA1C73525D89

In this Roadmap we find this kind of activity so early (instead in Realize) explains this SAP statement: *"The*

4.4 PREPARE

> *purpose of this task is to define and document the cutover strategy to move to SAP S/4HANA Cloud Private Edition. The cutover activities are executed on a very tight schedule. It is critical that the cutover strategy is defined early and well prepared to minimize the risk of delays later in the project."*
>
> The Accelerator **FP_45** is attached here

In the description, the following components of the strategy are listed:

- Cutover Approach
- Timeline
- Go Live Acceptance Criteria
- Cutover Organization and Responsibilities
- Cutover Schedule
- Cutover Simulations
- Cutover Communications
- Contingency Plan
- Implementation Support
- Logistics

> Activity: **Perform Data Volume Planning**
>
> https://go.support.sap.com/roadmapviewer/#/group//roadmap/a11ec6d657054bf9:FA163EAF25B21EEB8FC47DE9E72888DB/node/FA163EAF25B21EDB95A0184788107DBE
>
> This activity assigned to the data stream has impact on the Cutover. Properly realized data cleansing may shorten the downtime between the cutover and the cutover itself, as per the SAP statement: *"The purpose of this task is to plan and prepare the Data Volume Management (DVM). This task should be considered prior to a system conversion to reduce the amount of data to be converted. It can impact the duration and downtime of the cutover."*

There are attached Accelerators:
- **S4H_747 How to Approach Remote Cutover**
- **FP_45 Cutover Strategy**

Right after this node, there is another one with numerous cutover activities: **System Conversion Planning**

For the Roadmap: *SAP Activate Methodology for RISE with SAP S/4HANA Cloud Private Edition*

Activities Node: **System Conversion Planning**

This node groups 3 activities, all cutover related:
- Define Technical System Conversion Approach
- Define Conversion Cycles
- Define the Need of Dual Maintenance

Activity: **Define Technical System Conversion Approach**

There is attached Accelerator: Conversion Approaches and Downtime Optimization Techniques (Public)

Conversion Approaches and Downtime Optimization Techniques.pdf

https://support.sap.com/content/dam/SAAP/SAP_Activate/Conversion%20Approaches%20and%20Downtime%20Optimization%20Techniques.pdf

Activity: **Define Conversion Cycles**

https://roadmapviewer-supportportal.dispatcher.hana.ondemand.com/#/group/658F507A-D6F5-4B78-9EE1-0300C5F1E40F/roadmap/a11ec6d657054bf9/node/FABAD17D92534944BEEE8318908D7001

4.4 PREPARE

This is de facto Cutover mocking, which means exercising Conversion cycles to become proficient in the final Conversion during the Cutover.

There is attached Accelerator: Conversion Cycle Considerations and Risks (Public)

https://support.sap.com/content/dam/SAAP/SAP_Activate/Conversion%20Cycle%20Considerations%20and%20Risks.pdf

---

For the Roadmap: *SAP Activate Methodology for RISE with SAP S/4HANA Cloud Private Edition*

Task: **Define the Need of Dual Maintenance**

https://go.support.sap.com/roadmapviewer/#/group//roadmap/a11ec6d657054bf9/node/975019193E574212951E91C1CE646422:

This is in addition to the option to transit from ECC On-Premise to SAP S/4HANA in the Private Cloud via the System Conversion scenario.

Dual Maintenance is necessary if data have already been migrated for some time. However, the source system is still in use—a state that happens in some Pre-Cutover or Cutover scenarios.

Here I cite the purpose of the Dual Maintenance in this context: "*A conversion project can run for several months. During that time, the business may require changes to the production environment, prior to the final conversion, to continue successful operations. This may mean new configuration, code modifications or activating new functionality. The decision must be made how to apply these changes in the temporary SAP ERP landscape (N+1) and the production RISE S/4HANA landscape (Future N) prior to final Cutover of production to keep all the landscapes in-sync."*

There is attached Accelerator: Dual Maintenance Considerations and Risks (Public)

4.5 EXPLORE

I have found the two previously cited Roadmaps to be good references for Explore. In both cases, the roadmaps concern Test Planning and even exercise.

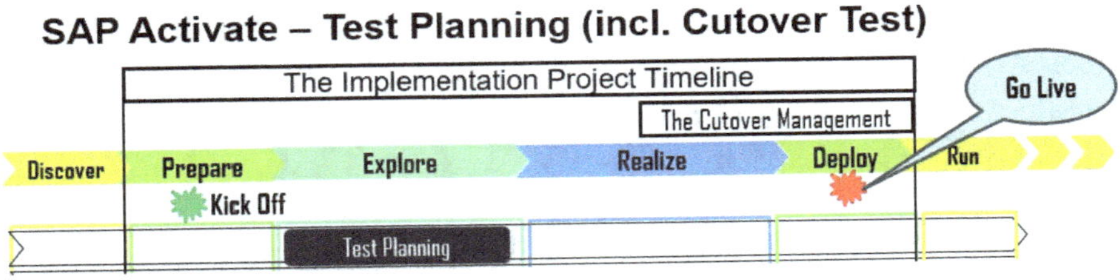

SAP Activate – Test Planning (incl. Cutover Test)

Figure 4.3: task Test Planning

4.5.1 Sap Activate Methodology For Transition To Sap S/4Hana

The Deliverable "Detailed Test Planning" in the Workstream "Testing " mentions Cutover test planning as part of the testing strategy.

> For the Roadmap: *SAP Activate Methodology for Transition to SAP S/4HANA*
>
> To scope and plan the tests for the project, whether it is a pure technical conversion, a combined conversion project with the enablement of new functionality, or a new implementation project.
>
> https://go.support.sap.com/roadmapviewer/#/group//roadmap/S4HANATRANSONPRE/node/001999B7BD851ED68D955DC097D2C2CE:

4.5.2 Sap Activate Methodology For Rise With Sap S/4Hana Cloud Private Edition

This Roadmap includes the Test Planning, the first conversion exercise, and the first Cutover test.

> For the Roadmap: *SAP Activate Methodology for RISE with SAP S/4HANA Cloud Private Edition*
>
> Activities Node: **Create and Schedule an Overall Test Plan**
>
> From the specification: *"Detailed test planning which covers tasks, dependencies, and durations that is integrated with the project plan should support the objective of mitigating risk both to the end-state solution and the **cutover** process required to position the end-state"*

Note also that a task, which is the facto about the Cutover, is located in the System Conversion path. The Conversion of the Sandbox must be seen as the first Cutover test in the project.

> For the Roadmap: *SAP Activate Methodology for RISE with SAP S/4HANA Cloud Private Edition*
>
> Activities Node: **System Conversion Execution of the Sandbox/Shell System**
>
> According to the specifications: *"This deliverable aims to run all the functional and technical activities needed to complete the conversion of the first sandbox system. After this conversion is finished, the project team must evaluate if they are ready to move to the productive landscape or if it is convenient to perform another sandbox iteration. As this first conversion cycle may reveal unknown issues/ activities, the project plan must be evaluated and adjusted*

> *accordingly depending on the potential impact"*
>
> The Accelerator attached is **CONV_OP2023.pdf**

Please also note that the list of tasks related to the test conversion is similar to Cutover Management (Preparation, Pre-Cutover, Cutover, and Post-Cutover), which is in practice:

- Document System Conversion Runbook
- Technical Pre-Conversion Activities
- Functional Pre-Conversion Activities
- Functional Pre-Conversion Activities: Finance Specific
- System Conversion Execution
- Execute Shell System Conversion
- Functional Post-Conversion Activities
- Functional Post-Conversion Activities: Finance Specific

This is also stressed in the Accelerator **Transition_to_SAP_S4HANA - 24Q1_Final** attached to this Roadmap, which calls straightforward conversion trials as refining the Cutover:

"Depending on the transport landscape configuration, there may be a need to perform multiple iterations of the conversion to solidify and finalize the <u>cutover plan</u>. Executing test migrations will validate the end-state of the conversion, as well as provide the figures for expected system downtime (see activity Downtime Optimization Preparation for details). Depending on the approach and the transport landscape configuration, there may be a requirement to execute additional sandbox conversions to optimize the <u>cutover procedure</u>."

4.6 REALIZE – START OF PREPARATION OF THE CUTOVER

In most roadmaps, the cutover preparation starts in the middle of Realize, and the preliminary cutover plan has to be accepted at the end of the phase.

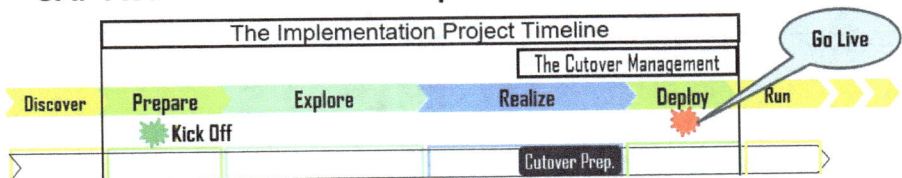

Figure 4.4: Cutover Preparation in Realize in most of the Roadmaps

The exception is in the "Transition..." roadmap, where the Cutover preparation is said to start at the end.

We will discuss some distinctions between paths to SAP S/4HANA within Roadmaps.

4.6.1 SAP Activate Methodology for Business Suite and On-Premise- Agile and Waterfall

The activity named here relates to the **Preliminary Cutover Plan** deliverable. The Preliminary Cutover Plan defines the approach and strategy, with timelines for The Cutover and Post-Cutover after the Go-Live.

The **Preliminary Cutover Plan** includes the high-level timing, steps, and logistics for the cutover; the following activities are named in Roadmaps as leading to the completion of this Deliverable:

- **Organizational Change Management Readiness Check**
- **Production Support Readiness Check**
- **Master Data Process Governance Readiness Check**
- **Preliminary Cutover plan and refining the Preliminary Cutover Plan with the Customer**

As we can see in the first item, the OCM is very closely bound to the Cutover, as with this process, the change in organization turns real. More you can find in:

For the Roadmap: *SAP Activate Methodology for Business Suite and On-Premise- Agile and Waterfall*

Task: **Preliminary Cutover Plan**

https://roadmapviewer-supportportal.dispatcher.hana.ondemand.com/#/group//roadmap/SUITEONPREMAGL/node/901B0E6D3F441EE8BFD346FD6D795863

List of subtasks above.

There is a task connected to the Data Migration stream:

For the Roadmap: *SAP Activate Methodology for Business Suite and On-Premise- Agile and Waterfall*

Task: **Legacy Data Migration**

https://roadmapviewer-supportportal.dispatcher.hana.ondemand.com/

#/group//roadmap/SUITEONPREMAGL/
node/901B0E6D3F441EE8BFD346FD6D799863:

The task aims to develop a detailed cutover sequencing plan and exercise data reconciliation and validation processes required to support the production cutover.

4.6.2 SAP Activate Methodology for Transition to SAP S/4HANA

There is a clear statement in the Accelerator **Transition_to_SAP_S4HANA - 24Q1_Final.pdf** making this Roadmap specific when it comes to the beginning of the Cutover Preparation:

'At the end of the Realize phase, the preparation for cutover starts. A cutover plan is created from experience gained in former transition runs (potentially additional mock runs are required).'

This Roadmap is specific because of the late start of Cutover Preparation, which can be explained by the fact that strategy and cutover testing were already set up earlier, before the "official" start.

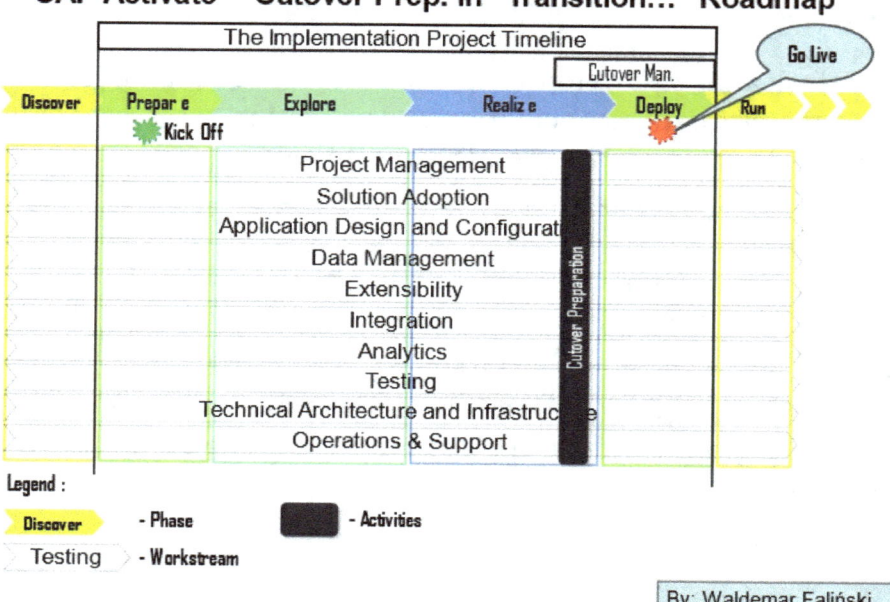

Figure 4.5: Cutover Preparation in "Transition..." Roadmap

It is also specific because it shows the Cutover activity again as common for all the Workstreams.

This Roadmap names all three paths, but since two, New Implementation and System Conversion, are quite consistent, the third one is a collection of various paths.

The path Selective Data Transition is the most complex...

...it may start with a new Implementation or System Conversion but later is a kind of another variant to some extent bearing characteristics of both but also have unique characteristics. This path is a set of various paths, thus tough to standardize.

This version is typical of roll-outs in waves for subsidiaries of multi-subsidiaries and multi-country transformations.

This Roadmap's names in Cutover preparation two tasks For the

New Implementation:

- **Production System Setup**
- **Create Cutover Plan**

The first task aims to provide a viable, correctly configured production environment for the project team to execute the final Go-Live simulation, which means the **Dress Rehearsal**. This is valid only for the New Implementation scenario.

After the Go-Live, this environment will be used as the future production system (PRD).

> For the Roadmap: *SAP Activate Methodology for Transition to SAP S/4HANA*
>
> Task: **Production System Setup**
>
> Deliverable: PRD environment ready for Go-Live simulation (the Dress Rehearsal)
>
> https://go.support.sap.com/roadmapviewer/#/group//roadmap/S4HANATRANSONPRE/node/001999B7BD851ED68D960013365AC2CE/001999B7BD851ED68D95DC673AFE62CE:t3,t1,t5

The second task here: "Create Cutover Plan," has three variants:

- Create a Cutover Plan (New Implementation)
- Create a Cutover Plan (System Conversion)
- Create a Cutover Plan (Selective Data Transition)

> For the Roadmap: *SAP Activate Methodology for Transition to SAP S/4HANA*
>
> Task: **Create Cutover Plan (New Implementation)**
>
> https://go.support.sap.com/roadmapviewer/#/group/AAE80671-5087-430B-9AA7-8FBE881CF548/

roadmap/S4HANATRANSONPRE/
node/001999B7BD851ED68D960013365BA2CE

This task is broken down into many atomic tasks. Please note this comment within its description: *"It is important to start the development of the cutover list early in the project. The list should be maintained by each workstream team throughout the Realize phase to avoid missing critical details."*

The following Accelerators are assigned to this task:

- How to Approach Remote Cutover (Public)

For the Roadmap: *SAP Activate Methodology for Transition to SAP S/4HANA*

Task: Create Cutover Plan (System Conversion)

https://go.support.sap.com/roadmapviewer/#/group//roadmap/S4HANATRANSONPRE/node/001999B7BD851ED68D9600FAD5C3A2CE:t1,t3,t5/001999B7BD851ED68D95DC673AFE62CE:t3,t1,t5

The Conversion scenario transitioning from SAP ECC to SAP S/4HANA is similar to the Upgrade, requiring a transition within the same SAP instance. However, conversion is much more complex than any standard upgrade, increasing the time pressure and making It challenging.

The following Accelerators are assigned to this task:

- How to Approach Remote Cutover (Public)
- SAP Value Assurance - Description of Services and Service Components (Public)
- Downtime-Optimized Conversion Approach of

SUM (Public)

- SAP Blog: System Conversion to SAP S/4HANA: downtime-optimized Conversion (Public)

For the Roadmap: *SAP Activate Methodology for Transition to SAP S/4HANA*

Task: **Create Cutover Plan (Selective Data Transition)**

https://go.support.sap.com/roadmapviewer/#/group/AAE80671-5087-430B-9AA7-8FBE881CF548/roadmap/S4HANATRANSONPRE/node/901B0E6D3F501ED6A3E808CF2E4F54B3

This task contains a long list of subtasks to execute and advice. Accelerator, a web page describing various variants of the Selective Data Transition scenario, is attached to this task (below).

Note: to access this Accelerator, the S-User is necessary!

Accelerator: **SAP Data Management and Landscape Transformation (DMLT) Homepage (Public)**

https://support.sap.com/en/offerings-programs/support-services/data-management-landscape-transformation.html

4.6.3 SAP Activate Methodology for RISE with SAP S/4HANA Cloud Private Edition

First, the activity Cutover Preparation is similar to what was already presented.

https://roadmapviewer-supportportal.dispatcher.hana.ondemand.com/#/group//roadmap/

a11ec6d657054bf9:FA163EAF25B21EEB8FC47DE9E728C8DB/node/FA163EAF25B21EEB8FC47E3B70ECC8DB

In this phase, there are also expected activities that influence the Cutover preparation:

- **Execute the System Conversion of the Development System**
- **Execute the System Conversion of the Quality System**

This then leads to the activity based on these and many more exercises (after the early in Prepare executed conversion of the Sandbox system): **Create the Cutover Plan for System Conversion**

For the Roadmap: *SAP Activate Methodology for RISE with SAP S/4HANA Cloud Private Edition*

Activity: **Create the Cutover Plan for System Conversion**

This activity takes the output from previously executed Conversion Cycle runs and provides the following steps (just some taken out of the list):

- Create a strategy document that includes the areas impacted by the cutover based on the **FP_45 Cutover Strategy.**
- Document critical.
- Assign all tasks and review the tasks with the owners to check the duration.
- Conduct at least one complete Dry Run of the plan as an entire team.
- Prepare the contingency plan.
- Work with owners of processes and batch jobs to safely and quickly ramp down and ramp up production operations.
- Find activities that can be completed ahead of time.

> To this activity the Accelerator is assigned: **FP_45 Cutover Strategy**

There are named following typically in the Cutover Plan:

- ʻ*Prerequisite steps for the production system conversion*
- *Ramp-down activities (e.g. batch jobs, interfaces, etc.)*
- *Pre-conversion validation reports*
- *End-user lockout*
- *Technical conversion*
- *Financial & Material Ledger data conversion*
- *Post-conversion changes (e.g. transports, parameter changes, etc.)*
- *Technical post-conversion validation reports (e.g. checking for business data consistency)*
- *Business-driven system validation and comparison of the pre-conversion and post-conversion reports*
- *Go/No-Go decision*
- *Ramp-Up activities (e.g. batch jobs, interfaces, etc.)*
- *Users unlock*ʼ

4.6.4 SAP Activate Methodology for New Cloud Implementations (Public Cloud-General)

For this Roadmap, there is the task:

> Task: **Cutover Preparation**
>
> https://go.support.sap.com/roadmapviewer/#/group/CD89F94E-618C-4C5C-BDD5-961451B9F5E0/roadmap/02c0b5bb07be485c98a3b3287f3b4cf1:1CA7E35E613040109F9469128BCC7273/node/53B8A394A0B940DA8B875BCE44523179
>
> It is worth mentioning that there is only one subtask, **Create Cutover Plan and Documentation**, with interesting specifications (I cite only the beginning below the section).

https://go.support.sap.com/roadmapviewer/#/group/
CD89F94E-618C-4C5C-BDD5-961451B9F5E0/
roadmap/02c0b5bb07be485c98a3b3287f3b4cf1:1CA7E
35E613040109F9469128BCC7273/
node/40042EEEA55B406F948FD4D88528BFA1/53B8A
394A0B940DA8B875BCE44523179

The following Accelerators are assigned here (see the Quick reference section for more):

Cutover Strategy Template.pptx (SAP Partner) - **FP_45 Cutover Strategy**

Cutover Template.xlsx (Public) - **S4H_403 Cutover Template**

How to Approach Remote Cutover (Public) - **S4H_747 How to Approach Remote Cutover**

Citation:

"Create Cutover Plan and Documentation

The purpose of this task is to develop and document the cutover plan for moving from the current (legacy) solution to the new solution and the post-go live support period. This includes the following activities:

- *Determining scope and timeline*
- *Setting up and initializing the production system*
- *Setting up and verifying interface connections and integrated applications*
- *Data migration*
- *User creation*
- *Closing the legacy systems*
- *Completing all required documentation for regulatory purposes (if required)*

- Planning timeline and meeting schedule for sequencing and simulating the cutover schedule

It is important that each team begin the development of the cutover schedule when starting configuration and maintain the list throughout the implementation to avoid missing critical details. Estimated durations should also be kept and refined so that the final schedule can calculated down to the minute."

4.6.5 Quality Gate at the end of Realize

The consequence of beginning the Cutover Preparation is that this is part of the Quality Gate.

The Quality Gate at the end of Realize first contains questions about the Cutover as per the Cutover Management main concept that starts here.

There are two Accelerators with closing criteria. The set of questions is pretty similar in both Accelerators.

I am bringing here the questions from the newest Accelerator **S4H_0271.xlsx**:

Criteria	Comment
The Deliverable is the preliminary cutover plan, which includes the high-level timing with steps and conditions for the cutover.	*Mandatory. All stakeholders should be involved in the preparation.*
Is the cutover strategy defined & signed off?	Question
Is a preliminary cutover timeline defined?	Question
Is a (draft) cutover plan/schedule available and reviewed with all stakeholders?	Question
What is the percentage of completion of the cut over plan and time remaining till dress rehearsal starts in next phase?	Question
Is a cut-over simulation planned?	Question

Are the criteria for "business readiness" defined and agreed?	Question
Are the criteria for "data readiness" defined and agreed?	Question
Are the criteria for "system readiness" defined and agreed?	Question
Are all impacted (business) processes identified and included in the cutover plan? Are needed tasks identified and incorporated?	Question

Table 4.1: The Cutover criteria in the Quality Gate at the end of Realize

4.7 DEPLOY – CUTOVER PREPARATION AND PRE-CUTOVER

Since Deploy is very Cutover focused and there are three stages of Cutover Management, I have also divided Deploy into three subchapters:

- Deploy – Cutover Preparation and Pre-Cutover
- Deploy - To-go Decision followed by the Cutover and concluding with the successful Go-Live
- Deploy - Post-Cutover (Post-Go-Live)

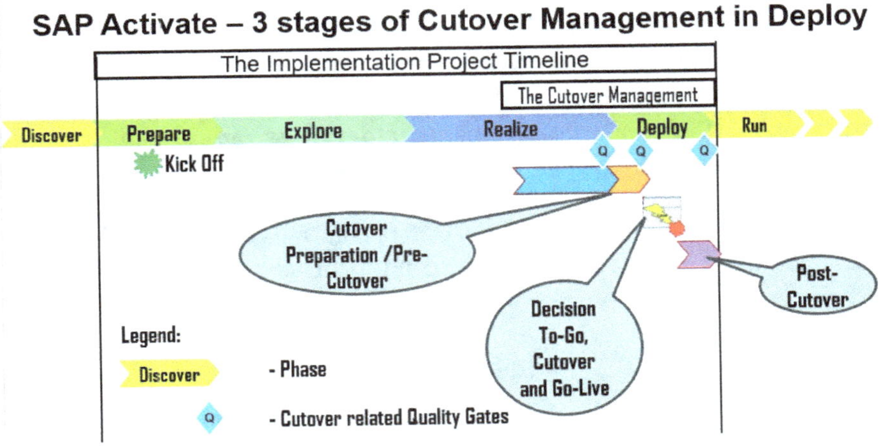

Figure 4.6: Three Stages of the Cutover Management in Deploy

Obviously, the Cutover Preparation in Deploy continues from the previous phase, Realize, but usually, the Quality Gate opens a way to some specific activities that may be classified as belonging to the Cutover itself, thus named Pre-Cutover, which can be recognized as belonging to Cutover Preparation.

Here again, the "Transition…" Roadmap is a kind of exception as it shows the Cutover stages as Cross-Workstream activities:

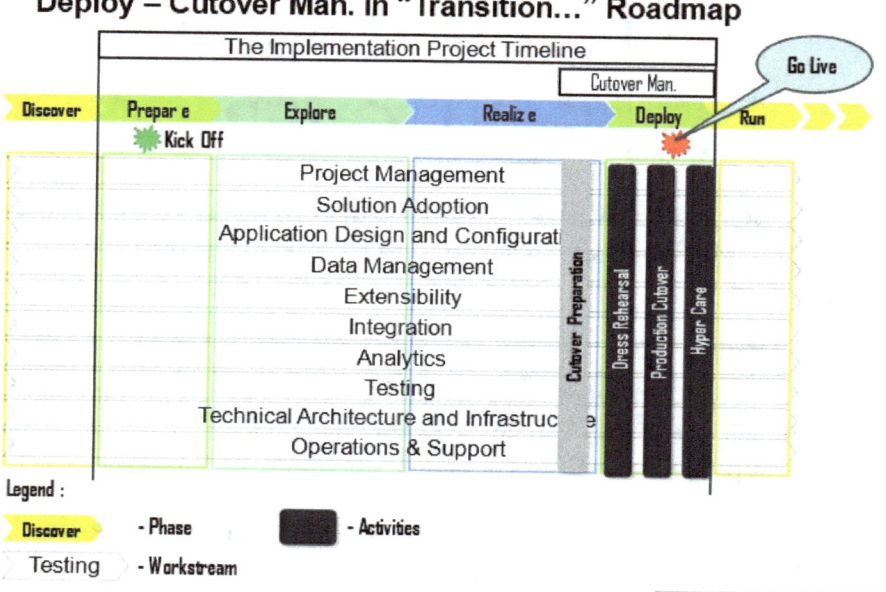

Figure 4.7: Cutover Management stages as presented in the "Transition…" Roadmap for the Deploy phase

The other Roadmaps position these activities in various Workstreams, so I would refer to the above figure as the right and most universal.

4.7.1 SAP Activate Methodology for Business Suite and On-Premise-Agile and Waterfall

4.7 DEPLOY – CUTOVER PREPARATION AND PRE-CUT...

There is a group of tasks related to the Cutover preparation.

> For the Roadmap: *SAP Activate Methodology for Business Suite and On-Premise- Agile and Waterfall*
>
> Task: **Organizational and Production Support Readiness Check**
>
> https://roadmapviewer-supportportal.dispatcher.hana.ondemand.com/#/group//roadmap/SUITEONPREMAGL:901B0E6D3F441EE8BFD346FD6D713863/node/901B0E6D3F441EE8BFD346FD6D7C3863
>
> I cite the description leading to set of sub-tasks:
>
> "*The purpose of this survey is to take the pulse of the organization, prior to go-live, to determine the general comfort level with the upcoming changes. If that comfort level is not there, it is critical to determine where additional OCM work needs to be focused. In addition the check of production support readiness is to ensure that the resources and processes are in place to support the solution after cutover.*"

However, note that many tasks usually classified as pre-cutover are already in this roadmap's "**Production Cutover**" section, thus discussed also in the next chapter:

- Execute Go Live Simulations 1 - n
- Conduct Data Quality Readiness Check
- Finalize Cutover Plan
- Perform Pre-Cutover Weekend Closing Activities
- Final Check of Production Readiness and Sign-Off

This is because this quite old Roadmap did not have an excellent Quality Gate right before the cutover, and the entire sequence "Pre-Cutover/Cutover/Post-Cutover" had barely the Quality Gate at the end of Realize.

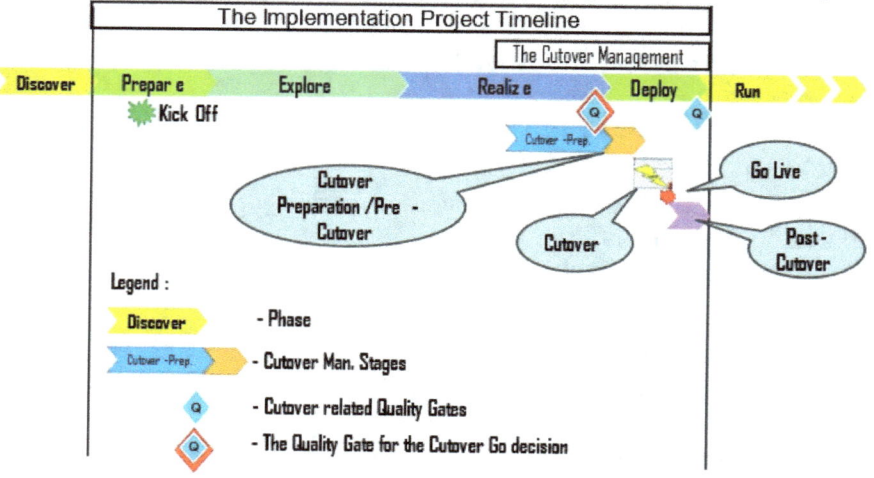

Figure 4.8: Cutover-related Quality Gate in older Roadmaps

4.7.2 SAP Activate Methodology for Transition to SAP S/4HANA

The assigned task here is '**Perform Cut-Over Rehearsal**'

> For the Roadmap: *SAP Activate Methodology for Transition to SAP S/4HANA*
>
> Task: **Dress Rehearsal**
>
> https://go.support.sap.com/roadmapviewer/#/group//roadmap/S4HANATRANSONPRE/node/001999B7BD851ED68D9730AD202AE2CE
>
> There are interesting prerequisites (citation):
>
> *"This activity is recommended for all scenarios.*

Prerequisite for this activity is:
1. *The detailed cutover plan with owners, dependencies and durations fully documented.*
2. *The involvement of all task owners.*
3. *A test environment representative of the source and target platforms for production.*
4. *The technical cookbook, which details all of the required technical migration steps."*

Sub-Task: **Perform Cut-Over Rehearsal**

https://go.support.sap.com/roadmapviewer/#/group//roadmap/S4HANATRANSONPRE/node/001999B7BD851ED68D973ED9020D82CE:

This task is intended to check the cutover process and, through practical exercises, familiarize all participants with how to execute their tasks and how long they last. It is supposed to be executed in an SAP Environment that possibly reflects the same scope and state as the target Environment for real Cutover and Go-Live.

Attached Accelerator: **S4H_747 How to Approach Remote Cutover**

Positioning Cutover Rehearsal so late is hardly feasible...

...if we consider that the complete environment can contain many other components besides SAP S/4HANA, placing this kind of complex and engaging many people, this task may be unrealistic in Deploy. In practice, the best is to perform the Cutover Rehearsal as part of UAT in Realize—this option I am supporting in my proposal for improved Cutover is described in the next part of this Guide.

4.7.3 SAP Activate Methodology for RISE with SAP S/4HANA Cloud Private Edition

This roadmap's activities align with all previous roadmaps, including the '**Dress Rehearsal**' task, which is similar to the above but with different specifications.

> For the Roadmap: *SAP Activate Methodology for RISE with SAP S/4HANA Cloud Private Edition*
>
> Task: **Dress Rehearsal**
>
> https://roadmapviewer-supportportal.dispatcher.hana.ondemand.com/#/group//roadmap/a11ec6d657054bf9:FA163EAF25B21EEB8FC47DE9E728E8DB/node/6D1AB76FC18240EF8C4A83E2D843EFE0
>
> Citation:
>
> *"The purpose of this deliverable is to validate the cutover procedure in preparation for the actual production cutover. The process includes:*
> - *Rehearsing of the cutover plan from end to end.*
> - *Identifying and mitigating risks.*
> - *Verifying completeness of steps.*
> - *Verifying sequencing and timing.*
> - *Validating dependencies.*
> - *Testing communications channels and plans both internal and external.*
> - *Verifying staffing needs.*
> - *Validating contingency plans."*
>
> There is a subtask, **Perform Dress Rehearsal**, with a description similar to the one above.
>
> Attached Accelerator: **S4H_747 How to Approach Remote Cutover**

4.7.4 SAP Activate Methodology for New Cloud Implementations (Public Cloud-General)

For this roadmap, there is nothing specific that adds to what was presented above.

4.8 DEPLOY-GO/NO-GO DECISION AND THE CUTOVER

Now, after all these steps leading to this, we are at the Cutover itself.

Often, the cutover begins with the Go/No-Go decision (like said, the negative variants are going to be elaborated in Part 5 of this Guide)

In all SAP Activate Roadmaps under the Deploy phase, there is a Quality Gate, with specific criteria grouped under Cutover Management that must be fulfilled as prerequisites before making the Go/No-Go decision. Once these are met, the Cutover process can begin.

4.8.1 Quality Gate Before the Cutover

This is the final Quality Gate before the Cutover, which ensures the project is ready for Go-Live and provides the basis for the Go decision.

4.8 DEPLOY-GO/NO-GO DECISION AND THE CUTOVE...

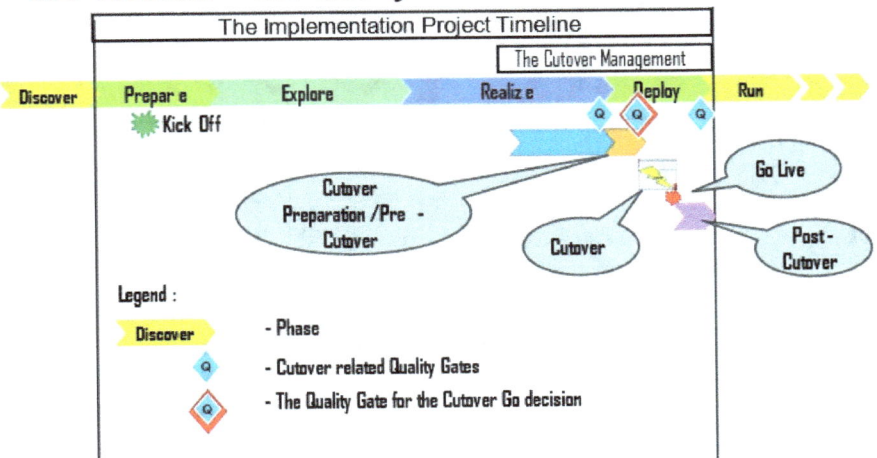

Figure 4.9: The Quality Gate commencing the Cutover execution

I am bringing here the questions from the newest Accelerator **S4H_0271.xlsx**.

Criteria	Comment
The deliverable for the final cut-over plan is an executable plan that communicates the timing, steps, and logistics to all parties involved. It includes the final cut-over schedule, communication, logistics, business, data & system readiness,	*Mandatory group of questions*
Is a final cutover timeline defined?	Question
Is a final cutover plan completed and signed off?	Question
Is the decision matrix clear and understood for the actual cut-over period?	Question
Are the go/no-go checkpoints planned?	Question
Is a contingency or fallback plan part of the cut-	Question

over plan?	
Is a data migration status part of the Cut-over plan?	Question
Has a cut-over simulation taken place?	Question
Are you ready?	Question
Is the business ready to go live?	Question
Is the data ready to go live?	Question
Is the system ready to go live?	Question

Table 4.2: The Cutover Management criteria in the Quality Gate at the end of Deploy

The following other Accelerators are assigned to this task:

- Quality Built In New QGate Checklist (Public) – **PM_211**
- SAP Activate Quality Gate Concept (Public) – **PM_210**

Now let's look at what is there in Roadmaps about the Cutover itself.

4.8.2 SAP Activate Methodology for Business Suite and On-Premise- Agile and Waterfall

As stated in the previous chapter, the older Roadmaps had no extra Quality Gate for the Cutover Go decision, and right after the end of Realize, the Deploy started with the group of tasks under the node "**Production Cutover**":

- Execute Go Live Simulations 1 - n
- Conduct Data Quality Readiness Check
- Finalize Cutover Plan
- Perform Pre-Cutover Weekend Closing Activities
- Final Check of Production Readiness and Sign-Off
- **Perform Cutover Weekend Activities**, Final Production Data Load
- Obtain Production Data Load Sign-off

4.8 DEPLOY-GO/NO-GO DECISION AND THE CUTOVE... 105

- ◆ Initiate Solution Manager Update - Solution Documentation

Please note that the first five are pre-cutover and cutover preparation activities, and the real Cutover is sixth on this list.

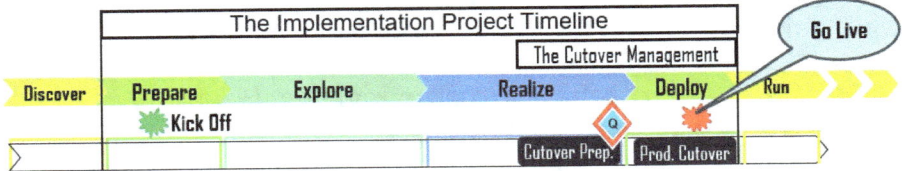

Figure 4.10: Cutover sequence in older Roadmaps

> For the Roadmap: *SAP Activate Methodology for Business Suite and On-Premise- Agile and Waterfall*
>
> Task: **Production Cutover**
>
> https://roadmapviewer-supportportal.dispatcher.hana.ondemand.com/#/group//roadmap/SUITEONPREMAGL/node/901B0E6D3F441EE8BFD346FD6D7CD863:
>
> Attached Accelerators: **FP_44.xls, FP_45 Cutover Strategy**

4.8.3 SAP Activate Methodology for Transition to SAP S/4HANA

Right after the 'Go' decision made at the Quality Gate, there is a task called '**Production Cutover**":

> For the Roadmap: *SAP Activate Methodology for Transition to SAP S/4HANA*
>
> Task: **Production Cutover**
>
> https://go.support.sap.com/roadmapviewer/

#/group//roadmap/S4HANATRANSONPRE/
node/001999B7BD851ED68D97325CC30222CE

This is a node with some content and links to three variants for every three SAP Activate paths to SAP S/4HANA, listed below:

Subtask: Convert Productive System (System Conversion)

https://go.support.sap.com/roadmapviewer/#/group//roadmap/S4HANATRANSONPRE/node/001999B7BD851ED68D974065E8E3A2CE/001999B7BD851ED68D97325CC30222CE

There is just a specified procedure listed:
1. *"Request Restore Point of Production System Prior to Final Cutover Activities*
2. *Execute the conversion of the production system following the tasks defined in the cutover plan.*
3. *Document the actual duration of each step to support future projects.*
4. *Capture any variances to the plan along with the decision maker who approved the change.*
5. *The cutover manager(s) should proactively notify task owners of upcoming tasks, to ensure their availability.*
6. *Regularly communicate status to stakeholders.*
7. *After conversion has finished (including mandatory post-processing activities), the system must be tested and validated*
8. *Obtain system sign-off"*

Subtask: Production Cutover (New Implementation)

https://go.support.sap.com/roadmapviewer/#/group//roadmap/S4HANATRANSONPRE/node/001999B7BD851ED68D974138C46842CE/001999B7B

D851ED68D97325CC30222CE

There is just a specified procedure listed:

1. *"Execute the cutover following the tasks defined in the cutover plan. This includes the final production data load.*
2. *Document the actual duration of each step to support future projects.*
3. *Capture any variances to the plan along with decision maker who approved the change.*
4. *The cutover manager(s) should proactively notify task owners of upcoming tasks, to ensure their availability.*
5. *Regularly communicate status to stakeholders.*
6. *After the data is loaded, testing and data reconciliation must be completed.*
7. *Obtain system sign-off"*

For these two paths, after the sequence of tasks there is a description, just a couple of lines, with the statement that after the customer approval (sign-off) documents the agreement with the stakeholders that cutover tasks have been executed, the go-live acceptance criteria have been met, and the cutover is finished. It indicates formal approval to end the cutover activities. At this point, **the solution is to live**.

In the case of the option of the Selective Data Transition, there is a bit more:

Subtask: **Production Cutover (Selective Data Transition)**

https://go.support.sap.com/roadmapviewer/#/group//roadmap/S4HANATRANSONPRE/node/901B0E6D3F501ED6A3E81AFEA09F14D8/001999B7BD851ED68D97325CC30222CE

Here, as this option has multiple scenarios there is a short description that this path may cover the following specific variants:

- Client Transfer
- System Merge
- Company Code Transfer
- Maybe including CVI and other objects on the fly
- Etc.

To this node again, the same as above, following Accelerator being a support page is linked:

Accelerator: **SAP Data Management and Landscape Transformation (DMLT) Homepage (Public)**

https://support.sap.com/en/offerings-programs/support-services/data-management-landscape-transformation.html

4.8.4 SAP Activate Methodology for RISE with SAP S/4HANA Cloud Private Edition

Here is the task '**Production Cutover**' with the sub-task '**Execute Cutover Tasks per the Cutover Plan**'

https://roadmapviewer-supportportal.dispatcher.hana.ondemand.com/#/group//roadmap/a11ec6d657054bf9:FA163EAF25B21EEB8FC47DE9E728E8DB/node/FA163EAF25B21EEB8FC47DE9E72968DB

For the Roadmap: *SAP Activate Methodology for RISE with SAP S/4HANA Cloud Private Edition*

Task: **Production Cutover**

https://roadmapviewer-supportportal.dispatcher.hana.ondemand.com/#/group//roadmap/a11ec6d657054bf9:FA163EAF25B21EEB8FC47DE9E728E8DB/node/FA163EAF25B21EEB8FC47DE9E72968DB

There is a short specification with a sequence of tasks (cite):

- *"Setting up and initializing the production system*
- *Setting up and verifying interface connections*
- *Migration or creation of master data*
- *Migration of order objects (i.e. purchase orders, sales orders, etc)*
- *User creation/access*
- *Go/no go decision points*
- *Closing the legacy systems*
- *Notification of impacted 3rd parties*
- *Completing all required documentation for regulatory purposes"*

There is just one of sub-tasks:

Subtask: **Execute Cutover Tasks per the Cutover Plan**

https://roadmapviewer-supportportal.dispatcher.hana.ondemand.com/#/group//roadmap/a11ec6d657054bf9:FA163EAF25B21EEB8FC47DE9E728E8DB/node/FA163EAF25B21EEB8FC47E3B70ECA8DB/FA163EAF25B21EEB8FC47DE9E72968DB

This contains the same sequence as already listed in the previous Roadmap (cite again):

1. *"Execute the cutover following the tasks defined in the cutover plan. This includes the final*

> production data load.
> 2. Document the actual duration of each step to support future projects.
> 3. Capture any variances to the plan along with decision maker who approved the change.
> 4. The cutover manager(s) should proactively notify task owners of upcoming tasks, to ensure their availability.
> 5. Regularly communicate status to stakeholders.
> 6. After the data is loaded, testing and data reconciliation must be completed.
> 7. Obtain system sign-off"

There is also a separate activity for the Go-Live:

> Task '**System Go-Live**'
>
> https://roadmapviewer-supportportal.dispatcher.hana.ondemand.com/#/group//roadmap/a11ec6d657054bf9:FA163EAF25B21EEB8FC47DE9E728E8DB/node/FA163EAF25B21EEB8FC47E07C6D108DB
>
> This task is just about confirming the PRD system is Live by communicating with all stakeholders.
>
> There is one sub-task: **Production System to Live**
>
> With a short procedure given (cite):
>
> > 1. "Ensure all project activities of the implementation project are set to 'Completed'.
> > 2. Confirm 'Complete Milestone Go-Live'.
> > 3. Execute Go-Live communications."

4.8.5 SAP Activate Methodology for New Cloud

Implementations (Public Cloud-General)

Subtask: **Execute Cutover Tasks per the Cutover Plan** https://go.support.sap.com/roadmapviewer/#/group/CD89F94E-618C-4C5C-BDD5-961451B9F5E0/roadmap/02c0b5bb07be485c98a3b3287f3b4cf1/node/0D3642B4E4EE45D3BB5309A72C2ED1B9/692E23AEE9A34A259B4FAE12BE802F55 These are again 7 tasks already cited in the last two Roadmaps. The following Accelerators are assigned here (see the Quick reference section for more): Cutover Strategy Template.pptx (SAP Partner) - **FP_45 Cutover Strategy** Cutover Template.xlsx (Public) - **S4H_403 Cutover Template** How to Approach Remote Cutover (Public) - **S4H_747 How to Approach Remote Cutover**

Just a mention, which is the consequences of the Public Cloud model:

- ◆ *"Planned system maintenance windows should be considered when planning data migration in order to avoid terminations. See product-specific maintenance schedules in the accelerator section.*

- ◆ *Relevant go-live tasks from integrated applications (BTP apps, Industry Cloud apps, third-party, etc.) are included in the cutover plan, resulting in a complete cutover list."*

4.9 DEPLOY - POST-CUTOVER (POST-GO-LIVE)

There are two groups of tasks we usually classify as Post-Cutover:

- Hyper-care
- Formal closure of the project

All roadmaps follow these two tasks, with some changes between them.

4.9.1 SAP Activate Methodology for Business Suite and On-Premise- Agile and Waterfall

For the Roadmap: *SAP Activate Methodology for Business Suite and On-Premise- Agile and Waterfall*

Task: **Production Support After Go Live**

https://roadmapviewer-supportportal.dispatcher.hana.ondemand.com/#/group//roadmap/SUITEONPREMAGL:901B0E6D3F441EE8BFD346FD6D713863/node/901B0E6D3F441EE8BFD346FD6D7BB863

This Task is the collection of the following subtasks aiming to ensure the stabilization of the newly implemented

4.9 DEPLOY - POST-CUTOVER (POST-GO-LIVE)

Business Solution (cite):

- *"Provide Post Go Live Support*
- *Monitoring Open Issues to Resolution*
- *Resolve Functional Issues*
- *Resolve Technical Issues*
- *Complete Transition to Customers Production Support organization*
- *Finalize Solution Manager Update - Solution Documentation*
- *Obtain Solution Transition to Production Acceptance Protocol Sign-off"*

Every one of these tasks has just a short description.

There is another task focused on formal project closure and handover to operation:

Task: **Project Closure and Sign-Off Project Deliverables**

https://roadmapviewer-supportportal.dispatcher.hana.ondemand.com/#/group//roadmap/SUITEONPREMAGL:901B0E6D3F441EE8BFD346FD6D713863/node/901B0E6D3F441EE8BFD346FD6D7BF863

The following sub-tasks are assigned to this node:

- *"Conduct Knowledge Management Gate*
- *Conduct Project Quality Gate*
- *Conduct Project Management Review Service*
- *Manage Fulfilled Contracts*
- *Resolve and close open issues*
- *Finalize Project Closeout Report*
- *Obtain Sign-off for Project Closure and Results Acceptance"*

4.9.2 SAP Activate Methodology for Transition to SAP S/4HANA

This roadmap groups tasks similar to the previous one, but the grouping of subtasks is different.

> For the Roadmap: *SAP Activate Methodology for Transition to SAP S/4HANA*
>
> Task: **Hyper Care Support**
>
> https://go.support.sap.com/roadmapviewer/#/group/AAE80671-5087-430B-9AA7-8FBE881CF548/roadmap/S4HANATRANSONPRE:001999B7BD851ED68BCCD7F18BA222CE/node/001999B7BD851ED68D9749B114A0A2CE
>
> Beside some specification there if the following sequence of tasks:
>
> - *"Monitor Resource Consumption*
> - *Analyze Workload*
> - *Check System Scalability*
> - *Follow-up on GoingLive Check (Verification Session)*
> - *Delete Obsolete Data with the "Obsolete Data Handling Tool"*
>
> Every one of these tasks has just a short description.
>
> Accelerators attached:
>
> - **SAP_VA_24Q3_SD.pdf**
> - **SAP Business Process Management and Improvement 24Q2_InfoSheet_FINAL.docx**

4.9 DEPLOY - POST-CUTOVER (POST-GO-LIVE)

There is another task focused strictly on the Handover based on resolved and closed incidents from the hyper-care:

> Task: **Handover to Support Organization**
>
> https://go.support.sap.com/roadmapviewer/#/group/ AAE80671-5087-430B-9AA7-8FBE881CF548/roadmap/ S4HANATRANSONPRE:001999B7BD851ED68BCCD7F18BA2 22CE/node/001999B7BD851ED68D974CF8D5B002CE
>
> Embracing two subtasks (cite):
>
> - Resolve and Close Open Issues
> - Handover Operations Responsibility

And another one about formal project closure:

> For the Roadmap: *SAP Activate Methodology for Transition to SAP S/4HANA*
>
> Task: **Project Closure and Sign-Off Project Deliverables**
>
> https://go.support.sap.com/roadmapviewer/#/group/ AAE80671-5087-430B-9AA7-8FBE881CF548/roadmap/ S4HANATRANSONPRE:001999B7BD851ED68BCCD7F18BA2 22CE/node/901B0E6D3F441EE8A0A4EF8024E14C95
>
> With the following subtasks (cite):
>
> - *"Conduct Knowledge Management Gate*
> - *Conduct Project Quality Gate*
> - *Manage fulfilled Contracts*
> - *Resolve and close open Issues*
> - *Finalize Project Closeout Report*
> - *Obtain Sign-off for Project Closure and Results Acceptance"*

Worth further diligence is the Conduct Knowledge Management Gate as this is about lessons learned as part of the Post-Cutover duties:

For the Roadmap: *SAP Activate Methodology for Transition to SAP S/4HANA*

Task: **Conduct Knowledge Management Gate**

https://go.support.sap.com/roadmapviewer/#/group/
AAE80671-5087-430B-9AA7-8FBE881CF548/roadmap/
S4HANATRANSONPRE:001999B7BD851ED68BCCD7F18BA222CE/
node/901B0E6D3F441EE8A0A4F10422DB4C99/901B0E6D3F441EE8A0A4EF8024E14C95

Attached Accelerators:

- ◆ Lessons Learned Guide (SAP Customer)
- ◆ Lessons Learned Template (SAP Customer)

4.9.3 SAP Activate Methodology for RISE with SAP S/4HANA Cloud Private Edition

This roadmap contains similar tasks but differently grouped:

For the Roadmap:

Task: **Production Hypercare Support**

https://roadmapviewer-supportportal.dispatcher.hana.ondemand.com/#/group//roadmap/
a11ec6d657054bf9:FA163EAF25B21EEB8FC47DE9E728E8DB/node/FA163EAF25B21EEB8FC47DE9E72E28DB

With just one subtask: **Provide Hypercare Support**

4.9 DEPLOY - POST-CUTOVER (POST-GO-LIVE)

Contains the following procedure (cite):

1. *"Review the SAP S/4HANA Cloud Private Edition - Roles and Responsibilities Summary accelerator, to understand the roles and responsibilities.*
2. *Establish a process for addressing adoption issues that end-users identify during the first days and weeks of using the system – leverage existing customer tools for IT ticketing.*
3. *Ensure business users know who to contact with questions – customer key business users should be available to help address adoption issues.*
4. *Define Business user issue-reporting and escalation processes."*
5. *Define and follow the process for raising SAP support tickets for software issues. Monitor the raised tickets and follow-up with SAP Support."*

Attached Accelerators (*Web Pages*):

SAP Cloud ALM for Operations (Public)

SAP S/4HANA Cloud Private Edition - Roles and Responsibilities Summary (Public)

Next one addressing the handover:

Task: **Handover to Support Organization**

https://roadmapviewer-supportportal.dispatcher.hana.ondemand.com/#/group//roadmap/a11ec6d657054bf9:FA163EAF25B21EEB8FC47DE9E728E8DB/node/FA163EAF25B21EEB8FC47DE9E72E48DB

Containing like in the previous Roadmap, two tasks:

- **Resolve and Close Open Issues**
- **Handover Operations Responsibility**

The last about Quality Gate and the closure of the project

> Task: **Phase Closure and Sign-Off Phase Deliverables**
>
> https://roadmapviewer-supportportal.dispatcher.hana.ondemand.com/#/group//roadmap/a11ec6d657054bf9:FA163EAF25B21EEB8FC47DE9E728E8DB/node/FA163EAF25B21EEB8FC47DE9E72E48DB
>
> Containing like in the previous Roadmap, the following tasks:
>
> ◆ *"Conduct Project Quality Gate*
> ◆ *Assess Project Performance*
> ◆ *Obtain Customer Sign-Off for Phase/Project Completion*
> ◆ *SAP S/4HANA Cloud Private Edition - Released Version September 23, 2024"*
>
> Accelerator assigned: **RISE with SAP S4HANA Cloud Private edition Release Notes**

4.9.4 SAP Activate Methodology for New Cloud Implementations (Public Cloud-General)

For this Roadmap, there is just one task being a node for two sub-tasks:

> Task: **Phase Closure and Sign-Off Phase Deliverables**
>
> https://go.support.sap.com/roadmapviewer/#/group/CD89F94E-618C-4C5C-BDD5-961451B9F5E0/roadmap/02c0b5bb07be485c98a3b3287f3b4cf1:FC8CC529775A48D7ACCE296D22197ABF/node/22F2024E314B4FBA89C03DE31B43515E

There are two sub-tasks:

- Project Quality Gate
- Sign-Off for Phase/Project Completion

4.9.5 Quality Gate Ending the project

So now we are at the final step of the project, at the Quality Gate, aiming to conclude the project as done, SAP Business Solution as successfully implemented, and to hand to the Business-as-Usual maintenance.

This fifth Quality Gate (in Accelerator **S4H_02710**) is named "Quality Gate 5 /Run—Transition to Support Organization." There are no sections or questions related directly to the Cutover, as this shall be done. All questions are about the project deliverables, thus confirming that the cutover is done.

4.10 RUN

The Run is already a post-project "phase," so this is a state of business as usual than any phase. That is why no project-related tasks are assigned here.

5 QUICK REFERENCE FOR CUTOVER ACCELERATORS

This Quick Reference will be structured as follows:

- Instruction on how to use the Quick Reference
- General learning content – Blog posts of SAP Activate Team, which are classified as Accelerators
- Cutover Accelerators
- Other Accelerators that refer to or touch the Cutover aspects
- Specific Blog posts being Accelerators for System Conversion
- Specific Blog posts being Accelerators for Selective Data Transition

Note: a specific group of Accelerators is available only for logged users via download, as described further, which is grouped in the next chapter, "Roadmaps and project plan templates".

5.1 HOW TO USE THE QUICK REFERENCE?

SAP Roadmap Viewer is a tool for accessing SAP Activates' knowledge and content, but its complex structure makes it challenging to find specific content or accelerators.

That is why I have compiled this Quick Reference list with a selection of accelerators to make it easier. This was a lot of work, and I am sharing it now to make it more accessible.

This list was very helpful to me, and I believe it can be beneficial for you as well.

The list of accelerators is organized by file names. There are two groups of Accelerators (may sometimes be both in one):

- Conceptual documents, which are handbooks, explaining the concept of using OCM within SAP Activate
- Templates to take and use - like OCM artifacts (documents, deliverables, etc.

Access to some components on the SAP Roadmap Viewer may require an "SAP S-user" for viewing and downloading. These are marked yellow.

However, most documents in this book are accessible even in anonymous mode—please refer to the disclaimer below.

The list in this Quick Reference has a rule-following structure:

◆ Title of the accelerator

◆ Name of file containing the accelerator and last date, some are created much sooner but I take the last indicated date, just as a snapshot at the time of writing as it may change

◆ Link to the accelerator you can click or copy to the browser

◆ My comment or citation from the document (in "") describing this accelerator.

You can click the link or copy and paste it into your browser's address bar.

There is a group of Accelerators; mostly, these are project plan templates and several guiding documents in the compressed ZIP files. Note that these accelerators are available only if logged in at least as the P-user available only via the download icon from the right-upper corner of the screen:

Figure 5.1: Snip from the SAP Roadmap Viewer with the icon to download the project plan template

5.2 GENERAL DOCUMENTS – BLOG POSTS BY SAP ACTIVATE TEAM MEMBER

As said, the SAP Community is a source of valuable information besides the SAP Roadmap Viewer. Here, SAP Activate subject matter experts publish blogs in the node "*Enterprise Resource Planning Blogs by SAP.*"

There, we can find a few documents that guide the Cutover.

Cutover Management: Planning and Orchestration
Blog post by Swastik
https://community.sap.com/t5/enterprise-architecture-blog-posts/cutover-management-planning-and-orchestration/ba-p/13693946
Interesting Blog about some aspects of the Cutover management
SAP Project Manager's Guide to SAP Project Cutover by former_member752547

https://community.sap.com/t5/enterprise-resource-planning-blogs-by-sap/sap-project-manager-s-guide-to-sap-project-cutover/ba-p/13510809?search-action-id=122486529701&search-result-uid=13510809

This Blog post explains the Cutover as an activity.

Lessons Learned: SAP ECC Systems Consolidation

By former_member227296, 2015

https://community.sap.com/t5/technology-blogs-by-members/lessons-learned-sap-ecc-systems-consolidation/ba-p/13274513

This blog post is already 9 years old but still valid. It provides an interesting case study of merging two systems into one. It discusses Cutovers, especially two separate cutovers (technical and business cutovers) and the business freeze caused by the cutover activities.

5.3 CUTOVER ACCELERATORS

Here are all accelerators that describe or at least touch the domain of the Cutover. The list is ordered alphabetically by file name.

This is because even if an accelerator is assigned to one phase, such as "preliminary" in Explore, it is usually valid in the next one as "final," etc. The Accelerator's name can also differ in the file and the Roadmap.

Conversion Cycle Considerations and Risks (Public)
Conversion Cycle Considerations and Risks.pdf
https://support.sap.com/content/dam/SAAP/SAP_Activate/Conversion%20Cycle%20Considerations%20and%20Risks.pdf
Document with 3 pages about Conversion cycles describes de facto the Cutover mocking, which means exercising Conversion cycles to become proficient in the final Conversion during the Cutover.
Conversion Approaches and Downtime Optimization Techniques (Public)
Conversion Approaches and Downtime Optimization Techniques.pdf
A document describing in the form of a diagram the possible

options for the conversion scenario.
https://support.sap.com/content/dam/SAAP/SAP_Activate/Conversion%20Approaches%20and%20Downtime%20Optimization%20Techniques.pdf
Dual Maintenance Considerations and Risks (Public)
Dual Maintenance Considerations and Risks.pdf
https://support.sap.com/content/dam/SAAP/SAP_Activate/Dual Maintenance Considerations and Risks.pdf
These are short—only 2 pages—documents that present considerations about the need for dual (parallel) maintenance in the Cutover scenario of transiting from SAP ECC On-Premise into SAP S/4HANA Private Cloud.
Please look at the Prepare part of the Roadmap Journey section sooner.
Cutover Communications
FP_44.xls, dated: 2018
https://support.sap.com/content/dam/SAAP/SAP_Activate/FP_44.xls
The template for the cutover communication plan is in MS Excel format. It has just headers without any prefilled content.
Preliminary Cutover Strategy Presentation Template (Public)
FP_45.ppt, dated February 14, 2023
https://support.sap.com/content/dam/SAAP/SAP_Activate/FP_45%20Cutover%20Strategy.pptx

R_169.ppt, dated September 9, 2021

[Template presentation for Cutover Strategy (with details becomes Cutover Kickoff).](#)

Two identical files of a Template with 25 slides for the Preliminary Cutover Strategy later turn into the Cutover Strategy and slide deck for the Cutover Kick-Off.

This content originates largely from ASAP. It covers many aspects, including Cutover Strategy with Timeline, Go-Live Acceptance Criteria, Cutover Organization Responsibilities of named cutover roles, Cutover Simulations, Communications, Contingency Planning, and team organization within business units.

[Data Migration Cutover Checklist](#)

FP_46.xls, dated 2018

https://support.sap.com/content/dam/SAAP/SAP_Activate/FP_46.xls

Template checklist of activities related to data migration cutover prefilled with data objects for Finance and HR. It aims to provide a structured and sequenced list of data migration-specific tasks that must be completed during the SAP cutover.

[Cutover schedule Template](#)

File: **FP_51.mpp**

https://support.sap.com/content/dam/SAAP/SAP_Activate/FP_51.mpp

MS Project template for cutover schedule Template, Accelerator is claimed as a Cutover plan, being de facto a

Cutover framework.
Lessons Learned Guide (SAP Customer) **PM_80.doc** https://support.sap.com/content/dam/SAAP/SAP_Activate/PM_80.doc A document with 6 pages – template of instruction how to collect and elaborate lessons learned.
Lessons Learned Template (SAP Customer) **PM_81.xls**, dated: 2017 https://support.sap.com/content/dam/SAAP/SAP_Activate/PM_81.xls A MS Excel template with instruction to fill in with lessons learned.
[Cutover plan](#) **R_168.mpp** https://support.sap.com/content/dam/SAAP/SAP_Activate/R_168.mpp MS Project file with more than 2000 lines of a sample for a multinational Cutover plan (day-wise) That comprises a sample of the Cutover plan in the MS Project format.
R_169.ppt is already presented together with **FP_45.ppt** above
[Playbook for Remote Cutover](#)

S4H_747 How to Approach Remote Cutover.pptx, Dated: May 14, 2020

https://support.sap.com/content/dam/SAAP/SAP_Activate/S4H_747%20How%20to%20Approach%20Remote%20Cutover.pptx

A document of 29 slides with exhausting explanations (comments also in the notes part of the file).

See the chapter about cutover management for a detailed description.

The Cutover Plan Template

S4H_403 Cutover Template.xlsx

https://support.sap.com/content/dam/SAAP/SAP_Activate/S4H_403 Cutover Template.xlsx

The Cutover Plan Template is in MS Excel format and has around 100 lines. For further details, please see the case study about this template further.

5.4 OTHER ACCELERATORS THAT TOUCH THE CUTOVER

Accelerators are not directly called for Cutover but are named in the Cutover-related activities in Roadmaps.

Test Strategy
BB_158.doc, dated: 2017
https://support.sap.com/content/dam/SAAP/SAP_Activate/BB_158.docx
The document is 58 pages long and describes all aspects of the test strategy. It contains a few mentions about cutover testing. Please refer to the Dress Rehearsal definition section above for more.
Conversion Guide for SAP S/4HANA 2023 (Public)
File: **CONV_OP2023.pdf**, dated: 2024-02-28
https://help.sap.com/doc/2b87656c4eee4284a5eb8976c0fe88fc/2023/en-US/CONV_OP2023.pdf
The 45-page guide explains the process of system conversion and includes many references to notes and other documents.

Project Closeout Presentation

GL_27.ppt, dated 2017

https://support.sap.com/content/dam/SAAP/SAP_Activate/GL_27.ppt

This is a template presentation with 15 slides for the project closeout report, a template for Project Management, but this is often considered the last of the Post-Cutover activities.

Project Charter

PM_15.doc, dated 2017

https://support.sap.com/content/dam/SAAP/SAP_Activate/PM_15.doc

Template of the Project Charter.

SAP Activate Quality Gate Concept (Public)

PM_210.pptx, dated January 18, 2024

https://support.sap.com/content/dam/SAAP/SAP_Activate/PM_210.pptx

A document with 27 slides combines the guide and the template for any presentation in the projects. It explains the concept of Quality Gates within SAP Activate in great detail, including how to prepare the QG Checklists and how to realize the QG meeting.

This document presents the Cutover Management as commencing in the middle of Realize and continuing to the very end of the project, which means the end of Deploy.

Quality Built In New QGate Checklist (Public)

PM_211.xlsb, dated 2017
https://support.sap.com/content/dam/SAAP/SAP_Activate/PM_211.xlsb
There is a newer version of this check-list in the Accelerator **S4H_0271.xlsx**
SAP S/4HANA Cloud Private Edition Release blog. File: **RISE with SAP S4HANA Cloud Private edition Release Notes** Dated: September 23, 2024 https://support.sap.com/content/dam/SAAP/SAP_Activate/RISE%20with%20SAP%20S4HANA%20Cloud%20Private%20edition%20Release%20Notes.pdf A document with 16 pages about the newest update in the Roadmap.
S/4HANA Quality Gate Checklist (Public) **S4H_0271.xlsx,** dated January 18, 2024 https://support.sap.com/content/dam/SAAP/SAP_Activate/S4H_0271.xlsx This is a new Excel template with tabs for 5 Quality Gates. The fourth is before the Cutover starts in the middle of Deploy, and the last (5th) is for the closure of Deploy, which is also the closure of the project. It has more than 100 questions/aspects per phase that must be considered at the end of every phase to conclude its closure.
SAP S/4HANA Conversion, Finance Part (Public)

S4H.0739 SAP S4HANA Conversion_ Finance Part.pdf
https://support.sap.com/content/dam/SAAP/SAP_Activate/S4H.0739%20SAP%20S4HANA%20Conversion_%20Finance%20Part.pdf
A comprehensive document for System Conversion addresses the Cutover in many aspects. It may be partially helpful for all scenarios.
SAP Value Assurance - Description of Services and Service Components (Public)
File: **SAP_VA_24Q3_SD.pdf**, Dated: 24Q3
https://support.sap.com/content/dam/SAAP/SAP_Activate/SAP_VA_24Q3_SD.pdf
A document containing 100 pages about measuring the results of the SAP implementation project.
Service Information – Service Components for Business Process Insights and Improvement (Public)
File: **SAP Business Process Management and Improvement 24Q2_InfoSheet_FINAL.docx**
Dated: 2021
https://d.dam.sap.com/a/K8uGnQn
A document with 3 pages about process improvements by using the SAP Signavio Business Process Transformation suite.

5.5 BLOG POSTS FOR SYSTEM CONVERSION AND OPTIMIZING THE DOWNTIME

Database Migration Option (DMO) of SUM - Introduction
By **Boris_Rubarth**
Use the Software Update Manager (SUM) database migration option (DMO) to simplify the migration steps.
DMO: downtime optimization by migrating app tables during uptime
By **Boris_Rubarth**
https://community.sap.com/t5/technology-blogs-by-sap/dmo-downtime-optimization-by-migrating-app-tables-during-uptime/ba-p/13108040
technique to further reduce the downtime of the Database Migration Option (DMO).
Downtime-optimized Conversion Approach of SUM

https://support.sap.com/en/tools/software-logistics-tools/software-update-manager/downtime-optimized-conversion-approach.html

5.6 SELECTIVE DATA TRANSITION AND LANDSCAPE TRANSFORMATION

[SAP Data Management and Landscape Transformation (DMLT) Homepage (Public)](https://support.sap.com/en/offerings-programs/support-services/data-management-landscape-transformation.html)

https://support.sap.com/en/offerings-programs/support-services/data-management-landscape-transformation.html

Link to Support pages with various variants of Selective Data Transition

6 ROADMAPS AND PROJECT PLAN TEMPLATES

Some accelerators are available only if logged in as at least the P-user, which, as I know, can get everyone interested by requesting at SAP.

These project plan templates, accompanied usually by some other interesting documents, are available only via the download icon from the right-upper corner of the screen while being in the roadmap and require additional "log in":

Figure 6.1: Snip from the SAP Roadmap Viewer with the icon to download the project plan template

6.1 SAP ACTIVATE METHODOLOGY FOR BUSINESS SUITE AND ON-PREMISE- AGILE AND WATERFALL

An **On-premise**, generic roadmap covering a wide range of possible SAP components implementation scenarios for the new implementation type.

https://roadmapviewer-supportportal.dispatcher.hana.ondemand.com/#/group//roadmapOverviewPage/SUITEONPREMAGL

In the case of this Roadmap, this package is also available via direct link: Project Plan Template (Public) https://support.sap.com/content/dam/SAAP/SAP_Activate/PM.210.zip

File: **PM_210.zip**, dated: February 2021

Contains:
- Project Plan Template in three formats MS Project, MS Excel, and SAP Solution Manager 7.2
- Document "2 SAP Activate Methodology Workstream Definition" containing 15 slides explaining the

concept of workstreams
- Document "3 SAP Activate Methodology for Business Suite and On-Premise - Agile and Waterfall - Overview Images" with Roadmap diagrams per phase.

The project plan template reflects the related Roadmap and contains cutover activities listed in the "Roadmap Journey..." chapter.

Note: According to SAP positioning, this roadmap is product agnostic, which means it is not directly related to any product (like SAP S/4HANA) and provides general and universal guidance and a set of accelerators mainly for the stream of project management.

6.2 SAP ACTIVATE METHODOLOGY FOR TRANSITION TO SAP S/4HANA

This Roadmap guides the project in the model On-Premise for all three transition paths to SAP S/4HANA.

https://roadmapviewer-supportportal.dispatcher.hana.ondemand.com/#/group/AAE80671-5087-430B-9AA7-8FBE881CF548/roadmapOverviewPage/S4HANATRANSONPRE

File: **PP_010.zip**, Last updated: 24Q1

Contains:
- **Project Plan Template** in three formats (MS Project, MS Excel, and SAP Solution Manager)—note that the MS Excel file also contains a list of all Accelerators with links.
- **Readme.pdf** – file with the description of the package.
- **Transition Roadmap Overview 24Q1.pdf** – file with graphical description of phases.

- **Transition_to_S4HANA_Roadmap_Version_24Q1** – file in two formats (pdf and ppt) again graphically showing the roadmap in details).

- **Transition_to_SAP_S4HANA - 24Q1_Final.pdf** – the comprehensive guide on 350 pages describing the SAP Activate method for this Roadmap.

Note the statement from the last document: *'At the end of the Realize phase, the preparation for cutover starts. A cutover plan is created from experience gained in former transition runs (potentially additional mock runs are required).'*

6.3 SAP ACTIVATE METHODOLOGY FOR THE INTELLIGENT ENTERPRISE

Cloud

This roadmap is designed to steer the project team through implementing business scenarios enabled by two or more SAP products integrated within the Intelligent Enterprise.

It embraces the following business scenarios:
- Hire-to-Retire
- External Workforce
- Source-to-Pay
- Total Workforce Management

Embraces:
- SAP S/4HANA Cloud
- SAP SuccessFactors
- SAP Fieldglass
- SAP Concur

https://roadmapviewer-supportportal.dispatcher.hana.ondemand.com/#/group//

roadmap/3f599fdbad8546d6/
node/901B0E6D3F441EE9B08A7B7490962FAB//overview

Project plan available via link: https://support.sap.com/content/dam/SAAP/SAP_Activate/S4H_209%20EM%20Project%20Plan.zip

(Also Contains Separate Project Plans For The Components That Are Connected With S/4Hana)

Project plan file: S4H_209 EM Project Plan (Excel and MS Project)

Last updated: February 2022

6.4 SAP ACTIVATE METHODOLOGY FOR RISE WITH SAP S/4HANA CLOUD PRIVATE EDITION

The SAP Activate Methodology in this roadmap is designed to guide the transition from SAP ECC On-Premise to SAP S/4HANA Cloud, Private Edition, with a focus on maintaining a clean core mindset, which is achieved through the **Fit-to-Standard** approach.

https://go.support.sap.com/roadmapviewer/#/group/658F507A-D6F5-4B78-9EE1-0300C5F1E40F/roadmap/a11ec6d657054bf9:FA163EAF25B21EEB8FC47DE9E72868DB/node/FA163ED752201EDBB5BB4FC89FAE85F9/FA163ED752201EDBB5BA9B0D95900434/overview

his roadmap covers all three transition paths: **System Conversion**, **New Implementation**, and **Selective Data Transition**.

There is no project plan template included.

Tip

According to SAP's positioning, although this roadmap is for the **Private Cloud**, it is also suitable for **On-Premise**.

6.5 SAP ACTIVATE FOR SAP S/4HANA CLOUD PUBLIC EDITION (3-SYSTEM LANDSCAPE)

Cloud

https://roadmapviewer-supportportal.dispatcher.hana.ondemand.com/#/group/658F507A-D6F5-4B78-9EE1-0300C5F1E40F/roadmapContentPage/82b2db84548d41209cda972f0fac428b:FA163ED752201EDABFE83D133CFD5D51,t27

Project plan template: **3SL.zip** (Excel and MS Project)

Contains its list of accelerators

Last updated: January 2024

6.6 BASELINE ACTIVATION SERVICE FOR SAP S/4HANA CLOUD (3-SYSTEM LANDSCAPE)

This is about activating only a baseline scope, which means what happens in the Explore phase. The scope included in this solution includes core business processes for Finance (Invoice to Cash, Invoice to Pay), Procurement (Invoice to Pay, Procure to Receipt), and Sales (Order to Cash). The scope is defined and can be extended by the customer in a subsequent phase.

https://roadmapviewer-supportportal.dispatcher.hana.ondemand.com/#/group/658F507A-D6F5-4B78-9EE1-0300C5F1E40F/roadmapOverviewPage/d9ffcd6438ab4ee9a02bfcf682502892

Project Plan Template: *PP_013 Baseline Activation Service Project Plan.xlsx*

last updated: February 2024

6.7 SAP ACTIVATE FOR SAP S/4HANA CLOUD PUBLIC EDITION (2-SYSTEM LANDSCAPE)

https://roadmapviewer-supportportal.dispatcher.hana.ondemand.com/#/group/658F507A-D6F5-4B78-9EE1-0300C5F1E40F/roadmapOverviewPage/IMPS4HANACLDENMGMT

Project Plan Template: **PP_001 S4HC ES Project Plan.zip** (contains Excel and MS Project files)

Contains a list of accelerators.

6.8 ORGANIZATIONAL CHANGE MANAGEMENT

https://roadmapviewer-supportportal.dispatcher.hana.ondemand.com/#/group/CD89F94E-618C-4C5C-BDD5-961451B9F5E0/roadmapOverviewPage/d605adcbf0c74812870d840a27972cc5

No accelerators for this roadmap

No project plan template

6.9 SAP ACTIVATE METHODOLOGY FOR NEW CLOUD IMPLEMENTATIONS (PUBLIC CLOUD- GENERAL)

This Roadmap is intended to guide the implementation team throughout the cloud implementation process for SAP Cloud solutions without specific roadmaps.

https://roadmapviewer-supportportal.dispatcher.hana.ondemand.com/#/group/CD89F94E-618C-4C5C-BDD5-961451B9F5E0/roadmap/02c0b5bb07be485c98a3b3287f3b4cf1/node/D50A4761B47740DDB331E1076FD417F5//overviewge

Project Plan Template: **PP_012** (only Excel version)

The project plan is only in MS Excel format and contains a list of accelerators.

last updated: 23rd February 2024

also available via: https://support.sap.com/content/dam/SAAP/SAP_Activate/PP_012.zip

This project plan reflects the Roadmap, and all Cutover mentions are the same as the Roadmap content.

Besides the above link, there is another project plan, with just two mentions about the Cutover:

S4H_209 EM Project Plan

6.10 SAP Activate for Upgrade of SAP S/4HANA Cloud Public Edition (3-system landscape)

https://go.support.sap.com/roadmapviewer/#/group/1B9D1B79-D03B-42F6-937C-08DE7C252BB6/roadmapOverviewPage/b6cc8dc5bbb749a59e1e21a4796c796f

Project Plan Template: PP_17 (only Excel version)

last updated 27th January 2022

6.11 SAP ACTIVATE METHODOLOGY FOR SAP S/4HANA UPGRADES

Those running SAP S/4HANA who need to upgrade to the newest releases. Embraces two upgrade approaches and the integration of embedded solutions are described in this transition roadmap: Technical upgrades and Functional upgrades

https://roadmapviewer-supportportal.dispatcher.hana.ondemand.com/#/group/1B9D1B79-D03B-42F6-937C-08DE7C252BB6/roadmapContentPage/MATS4HANA:901B0E6D3F501ED7A3E293999BC38275,901B0E6D3F501ED7A3E2945C40E7C275,901B0E6D3F501ED7A3E2956696C40275,901B0E6D3F501ED7A3E2964DFC4D027A,901B0E6D3F501ED7A3E297651817427A,901B0E6D3F501ED7A3E298058F67027A

project plan templates:

https://support.sap.com/content/dam/SAAP/SAP_Activate/AGS_48.zip

7 OTHER USEFUL LINKS WITHIN THE SAP UNIVERSE

- SAP Activate Roadmap Viewer

https://roadmapviewer-supportportal.dispatcher.hana.ondemand.com/

- SAP Support Portal

https://support.sap.com/en/index.html

- SAP Activate Methodology Community

https://community.sap.com/topics/activate

- SAP Signavio Process Navigator

https://me.sap.com/processnavigator/HomePage

- SAP Help Portal

http://help.sap.com/s4hanacloud

- SAP Central Business Configuration

https://help.sap.com/viewer/product/CENTRAL_BUSINESS_CONFIGURATION/2021_05/en-US

- SAP Cloud ALM Support Site

https://support.sap.com/en/alm/sap-cloud-alm.html

- SAP Influence Portal

https://influence.sap.com/saps4hanacloud

- SAP S/4HANA Cloud Implementation Learning Room

https://performancemanager.successfactors.eu/sf/learning?Treat-As=WEB&bplte_company=learninghub&_s.crb=eRDbzxBTaAGIN9mln%2bmumqMwgdQ%3d

- SAP S/4HANA Cloud Blogs

https://www.sap.com/community/tag.html?id=67837800100800007389&tag=type:blog

- SAP S/4HANA Cloud Customer Community

https://s4hanacloud.community.sap/

ABOUT THE AUTHOR

Waldemar Faliński

I am a Master of Science and Engineer in Electronics and a Doctor of Economics, specializing in Business IT Systems.
I have worked in the SAP domain for over 25 years, holding various positions such as Product Director at SAP Pl, Support Manager, SAP Project Manager, Roll-Out Manager, Delivery Manager, and Cutover Manager.

I graduated from the Technical University in Wrocław with an Engineer's degree in Electronics and a Master of Science and Engineering in Electronics, specializing in Information Systems. This gave me a solid technical foundation in Information Technology.

Afterward, I became a researcher and lecturer at the Business University in Wrocław. My research at the Institute of Management Systems focused on the "soft side" of IT, exploring methodologies and improving effectiveness. I earned a Doctorate in Economics, specializing in Business IT Systems.

In 1994, I began supporting SAP in establishing its subsidiary in Poland. Initially, I worked as a Finance Consultant, translating the FI module into Polish and promoting SAP in the local market. Formally, I held the position of Product Development Manager, leading a team responsible for adapting the SAP R/3 system to meet local requirements. In 1995, I decided to pursue academia and focus entirely on business.

During the first decade of my SAP career, I was employed at SAP PL. I focused on local business development, managed and oversaw SAP projects for new customers, and executed multiple roll-outs for international companies. In 2004, I left SAP PL and began working as a contractor for various integration vendors and end customers, including SAP.

One of the key challenges at that time was ensuring the SAP system complies with Polish accounting laws. I led a project that resulted in a recommendation from the Polish Association of Accountants for SAP R/3, eliminating any controversies about the system's legal compliance.

2004, I officially left SAP but continued working for SAP PL as an external service provider.

Since then, I have been involved in dozens of SAP implementations. As an SAP implementation expert, I have contributed to marketing strategies, conducted audits, and participated in presales activities.

I occasionally lecture at universities and provide ACT100 and ACT200 (standard SAP Activate methodology) training at the SAP Training Center.

Recently, I achieved a personal milestone by writing and publishing books, the first of which was launched in July 2024.

I firmly believe that while digital technology creates valuable opportunities for new business architectures, the organization —the people within it—must ultimately drive the necessary changes to fully realize those opportunities.

I am actively involved in sharing best practices and enjoy working on digital transformation projects. I also value engaging with social networks, students, and peers, which keeps me connected to the broader community.